HOW JESUS
RUNS
THE
CHURCH

GUY PRENTISS WATERS

P&R
PUBLISHING
P.O. BOX 817 • PHILLIPSBURG • NEW JERSEY 08865-0817

Library of Congress Cataloging-in-Publication Data

Waters, Guy Prentiss, 1975-
  How Jesus runs the church / Guy Prentiss Waters.
     p. cm.
  Includes bibliographical references and indexes.
  ISBN 978-1-59638-252-7 (pbk.)
  1. Presbyterianism. 2. Church polity--Biblical teaching. 3. Presbyterian Church in America--Government. I. Title.
  BX9190.W38 2011
  262'.051--dc23
                          2011016914

To my children:

Phoebe Louise Waters

Lydia Anne Waters

Thomas Edward Elzberry Waters

May the church and the church's only Head, Jesus Christ,
be precious to you all your days

CONTENTS

FOREWORD

For about a decade, I taught a course on Presbyterian ecclesiology and worship at Gordon-Conwell Theological Seminary. I developed a fairly extensive bibliography (nineteen pages, single-spaced), and was surprised at how much had been written about the church (*ecclesiology*) in the seventeenth to nineteenth centuries, and how little since then. One result is that even if someone were interested in learning more about Christ's church, it would be hard to do so without the resources of a theological seminary, since most of the good material written about the church was out of print. Thomas E. Peck (the successor to Robert Lewis Dabney at Union Seminary in Virginia) was out of print; Princeton's Charles Hodge recorded most of his ecclesiastical writings in the *Princeton Theological Review*; Charleston's Thomas Smyth was out of print; Edinburgh's James Bannerman was in and out of print; John B. Adger hid himself in the pages of the *Southern Presbyterian Review* (1847–85).

The seventeenth to nineteenth centuries had addressed matters not only thoroughly but avidly. In 1841, Thomas Smyth wrote *An Ecclesiastical Catechism* that took up 124 pages and asked and answered 280 questions related to the church, such as these:

- "What is the meaning of the word *catholic*?"
- "In what then does the unity of the church essentially consist?"
- "What do you mean by a true church?"

- "Is a connexion with any visible church, sufficient to secure the salvation of the soul?"
- "What further is the duty of the members of each particular church, toward those of every other Christian denomination?"

Today, we would be hard pressed to think of 280 questions to raise about the church, and even harder pressed to find anyone who could answer them.

Some things of a more recent nature had been written about the church, but they were prevailingly practical: how to organize meetings, how to deal with youth (and their parents!), how to counsel people who wanted none of it, and so forth. But the questions of how the church ought to be governed, by whom, and to what ends were largely unaddressed. What, if any, kind of power does the church have? What kinds of things may its officers rightly require of the members? Is membership itself important, or necessary, or an aspect of Christian discipleship? These questions were not being answered wrongly; they simply were not being asked at all.

On occasions, these (and like) questions were eventually raised in circumstances in which ecclesiastical catastrophe had already occurred. In churches that had suffered terrible, painful divisions (or gone under altogether), the survivors sometimes asked whether the pain could have been avoided, and if so, how. But by and large, thoughtful works on the nature of the church, and her government and its limits, were simply not being addressed.

Into this arid desert Dr. Guy Waters has inserted an oasis. In a book that is equally thorough yet brief, learned yet accessible, nuanced yet clear, Dr. Waters has covered the bases of ecclesiology with his *How Jesus Runs the Church*. His work is historically informed, theologically integrated, and biblically grounded; his discussions of controverted matters are always fair-minded and judicious. While not everyone will be capable of agreeing with him on every smaller point, everyone will find that he fairly and charitably engages those views with which he disagrees. If this book had existed when I was teaching at Gordon-Conwell, we would not have worn out the photocopier reproducing chapters and articles from old books and journals.

In a narcissistic, egalitarian, plurastic, and voluntaristic American culture, Dr. Waters's careful discussion of the way the risen Christ rules his church may seem as peculiar as my Greek lectures; but it is precisely what we need, and what we have needed for a long time. There are only two kinds of people who should read this book: those who love Christ's bride, the church, and those who do not.

T. David Gordon
Professor of Religion and Greek
Grove City College
Grove City, Pennsylvania

ACKNOWLEDGMENTS

I am a Presbyterian but not the son of a Presbyterian. Raised in the Lutheran church, I formally entered the Presbyterian Church in America later in life—at the ripe old age of twenty. I relished then (and still do) the PCA's unswerving commitments to biblical authority and to the Reformed faith. I confess, however, to an early bewilderment at Presbyterian polity. "Elder," "deacon," "court," "session"—these were just a few of the unfamiliar terms that I encountered as a new Presbyterian. I was counseled to purchase a copy of the PCA's *Book of Church Order*. I did so and began to study it. Some of my questions were answered. Even more questions were raised. I have always liked knowing how things work, and why they work the way that they do. I wanted to know how and why we Presbyterians do what we do in the government of the church. Where could I go to start getting some answers?

I did not know it at the time, but that curiosity was the seed from which this book would germinate into its present form. Along the way, I have had a lot of help. It was David F. Coffin Jr. who first pointed me to some of the classic statements and expositions of Presbyterian church government. This material has not always been easy to locate, but its rewards have far excelled my expectations. I have been able to sit in on a sustained conversation of some of the finest Reformed minds of the past four centuries. This has been a privilege indeed. So much so that I wanted to give twenty-first-century readers an opportunity to "listen in" with me.

Rare is the living individual for whom church government ignites keen interest, much less passion. In God's providence, I have encountered a few along the way. I am particularly grateful to Dave Coffin, J. Ligon Duncan III, James "Bebo" Elkin, David Jussely, and W. Duncan Rankin for profitable conversation and counsel in this area. I must also extend thanks to Bebo, C. N. Willborn, and T. David Gordon, each of whom has generously given of his time to read a draft of this work and to provide feedback. T. David was kind enough to supply a foreword to this book, and for that I am especially appreciative.

Presbyterian church government must be learned but it must also be modeled. I am grateful for some good models over the years. The ministers and elders of the Church of the Good Shepherd (PCA), Durham, North Carolina, where I had the opportunity to serve as an intern, showed me how well-functioning church government could benefit the life of the congregation. The Mississippi Valley Presbytery (PCA), in whose midst I serve as a teaching elder in the PCA, has done the same for me on a broader scale.

The institution at which I teach, Reformed Theological Seminary, Jackson, graciously gives me the opportunity to teach a course on church polity each year. Robert C. Cannada Sr., a founding father of the PCA and one of the founders of RTS, had particular interest in Presbyterian church government. W. Jack Williamson, another founding father of the PCA, taught church polity at RTS-Jackson for many years until he went home to be with the Lord. This is quite a legacy, and I take up the responsibilities of this course with some awe and trepidation. For their continued support and encouragement, I must especially thank Dr. Guy Richardson, President of Reformed Theological Seminary, Jackson, and Dr. Miles Van Pelt, Academic Dean of Reformed Theological Seminary, Jackson.

I am grateful to my polity students on whom I field tested the material in this book. Their questions, comments, and reflections helped me to sharpen and to refine my thoughts. I trust that this book is the better for it. Particular thanks must go to my research assistant, Michael Lynch, who diligently read and helpfully commented on this work in draft form.

Special thanks go to Marvin Padgett, vice president-editorial at P&R Publishing. This project would not have seen the light of day but for his encouragement and support. I am also grateful to the rest of the team at P&R for their collective labors in connection with this book. I wish particularly to thank John J. Hughes, who oversaw the editing process to completion; Rick Matt, who copyedited the work; and Mary Ruth Murdoch, who proofread the work.

I must reserve final thanks to my family. My wife, Sarah, has been behind me all the way, extending nothing but loving support and encouragement. My children are just getting to the ages where they can understand what biblical church government is. I hope one day that they will, and then embrace it as the good gift of Jesus to his church. In fact, that is what I hope that you will do as well. May the Lord be pleased to use this book to that end.

Guy Prentiss Waters
Jackson, Mississippi
February 2011

ABBREVIATIONS

BCO   *The Book of Church Order of the Presbyterian Church in America*, 6th ed. (Lawrenceville, GA: Office of the Stated Clerk of the Presbyterian Church in America, 2010)

NICNT   New International Commentary on the New Testament series, published by Eerdmans

RAO   Rules of Assembly Operations: With Revisions Adopted by the 38th General Assembly, 2010; distributed with *The Book of Church Order of the Presbyterian Church in America* (Lawrenceville, GA: Office of the Stated Clerk of the Presbyterian Church in America, 2010)

SCSEE   Studies in Christian Social Ethics and Economics series, published by Acton Institute

WCF   Westminster Confession of Faith, in *Westminster Confession of Faith* (Glasgow: Free Presbyterian Publications, 1958)

WLC   Westminster Larger Catechism, in *Westminster Confession of Faith* (Glasgow: Free Presbyterian Publications, 1958)

WSC   Westminster Shorter Catechism, in *Westminster Confession of Faith* (Glasgow: Free Presbyterian Publications, 1958)

INTRODUCTION

What comes to mind when you hear the word "government"? In the United States, most citizens have regular contact with local, state, and federal government. Sometimes the government makes demands on our time, like jury duty or military service. At other times, the government makes demands on our pocketbooks, like sales taxes; and on our paychecks, like income taxes. It is common to hear people complain about the demands that their elected representatives make upon them.

It is also easy to forget the good things that well-functioning government provides for its citizens. Schools, roads, public safety, and a host of other services and benefits make it possible for you and me to go to work, to raise our families, and to gather with God's people for worship and service. If you have ever visited or lived in a country with poor or dysfunctional government, you can truly appreciate good government. Poor government can mean that we cannot count on such things as stable jobs, clean water and electricity, or personal security. Poor government can even mean that citizens cannot enjoy the basic liberties and freedoms that many of us in the West enjoy. In short, whether we think about government much or not, government makes a big difference in the quality of our day-to-day lives.

GOVERNMENT IN THE CHURCH

The church has a government of its own. This is no accident. As we will see, the Scriptures teach that Jesus himself has instituted a government for his church, a government that we find in the Bible and in the Bible alone. This government is an important part of the way that Jesus rules his people.

Like civil government, the government of the church can sometimes make demands upon us. Also like civil government, well-functioning church government helps the people of God to live their Christian lives well. When church government ceases to be what Jesus has called her to be, that breakdown can hurt Christian living.

Church government, in other words, is a critical part of Christian discipleship. The government of the church is something in which every Christian should have keen interest. Whether you are a young Christian or a mature Christian; new to a Presbyterian church, or descended from generations of Presbyterians; a non-officer or an experienced church officer—you need to know what the Bible teaches about church government. This knowledge will help you to pursue a fruitful Christian life, to pray better for the officers and the work of the church, and to serve the church more capably. Above all, it will help you to have renewed appreciation for the wisdom and the glory of the church's only Head and King, Jesus Christ.

WHAT HAPPENED TO CHURCH GOVERNMENT?

It is fair to say that interest in church government (also called church polity) has waned in the last century. One way to see this is by looking at publications concerning church polity. Although they have been reprinted, the classic articulations of Presbyterian church government by Thomas E. Peck, Thomas Witherow, and John Macpherson date from the nineteenth century.[1] Classic Presbyterian treatments of the doctrine of the church likewise date from the same period.[2] This is

---

1. Thomas E. Peck, *Notes on Ecclesiology* (Richmond, VA: Presbyterian Committee of Publication, 1892; repr., Greenville, SC: Presbyterian Press, 2005); Thomas Witherow, *The Apostolic Church: Which Is It? An Enquiry at the Oracles of God as to Whether Any Existing Form of Church Government Is of Divine Right*, 5th rev. ed. (1881; repr., Glasgow: Free Presbyterian Publications, 1990); John Macpherson, *Presbyterianism* (Edinburgh: T&T Clark, 1882). An edition of this last work was printed as late as 1949.

2. Representative are Stuart Robinson, *The Church of God as an Essential Element of the Gospel* (Philadelphia: Joseph M. Wilson, 1858; repr., Willow Grove, PA: The Committee on

not to speak of the countless articles, reviews, and speeches that were published in the journals, newspapers, minutes, and other organs of nineteenth-century Presbyterian bodies.[3]

These manuals, books, articles, and speeches reflect vigorous discussions and, at times, disagreements among nineteenth-century Presbyterians about church government. They remind us of a time when some of the best and brightest ministers and theologians of the Presbyterian church devoted their time and energy to questions of church polity.

Nor was this concern and devotion unique to the nineteenth century. Book IV of Calvin's 1559 *Institutes of the Christian Religion*—a full third of the *Institutes*—is devoted to the doctrine of the church.[4] A substantial portion of Book IV addresses questions relating to the government of the church. This concern was carried over to sixteenth- and seventeenth-century Scotland, where John Knox, Samuel Rutherford, and George Gillespie reflected extensively on the government of the church.[5] In keeping with her Reformation and Scottish Presbyterian

Christian Education of the Orthodox Presbyterian Church, 2009); James Bannerman, *The Church of Christ: A Treatise on the Nature, Powers, Ordinances, Discipline, and Government of the Christian Church,* 2 vols. (Edinburgh: T&T Clark, 1868; repr., Edinburgh: Banner of Truth, 1960); Thomas Witherow, *The Form of the Christian Temple: Being a Treatise on the Constitution of the New Testament Church* (Edinburgh: T&T Clark, 1889); William D. Killen, *The Framework of the Church: A Treatise on Church Government* (Edinburgh: T&T Clark, 1890).

3. A handful of these were gathered and given more permanent form. See Robert L. Dabney, *Discussions: Evangelical and Theological,* vol. 2 (Richmond, VA: Presbyterian Committee of Publication, 1891; repr. Edinburgh: Banner of Truth, 1967); James H. Thornwell, *Collected Writings of James Henley Thornwell,* vol. 4: *Ecclesiastical,* ed. John B. Adger and John L. Girardeau (Richmond, VA: Presbyterian Committee of Publication, 1873; repr., Edinburgh: Banner of Truth, 1974); Thomas E. Peck, *Miscellanies of Thomas E. Peck,* 3 vols. (Richmond, VA: Presbyterian Committee of Publication, 1895–97; repr., Edinburgh: Banner of Truth, 1999); Charles Hodge, *Discussions in Church Polity: From the Contributions to the "Princeton Review"* (New York: Charles Scribner's Sons, 1878).

4. John Calvin, *Institutes of the Christian Religion,* 2 vols., ed. John T. McNeill, trans. Ford Lewis Battles, Philadelphia: Westminster, 1960), 1009–521.

5. John Knox, *Second Book of Discipline* (1578), repr. in Robinson, *The Church of God,* 117–49; Samuel Rutherford, *A Peaceable and Temperate Plea for Paul's Presbytery in Scotland* (1642); *The Due Right of Presbyteries* (1644); *Divine Right of Church Government and Excommunication* (1646); George Gillespie, *Treatise of Miscellany Questions, Aaron's Rod Blossoming . . ., 111 Propositions on Church Government, Assertion of the Government of the Church of Scotland, and Dispute against the English-Popish Ceremonies Obtruded upon the Church of Scotland,* repr. in *The Presbyterian's Armoury,* 3 vols. (Edinburgh: R. Ogle and Oliver and Boyd, 1846).

heritage, the American Presbyterian church maintained the Reformed church's longstanding concern with the doctrine of the church, generally, and church polity, specifically.

Presbyterians today, of course, continue to study, discuss, and debate the government of the church.[6] We do not do so, however, to the degree that previous generations once did. This raises two related questions. Why has this interest waned? Why was church polity so important to our Presbyterian fathers?

One important reason interest in church polity has waned is because of the sad experiences of many conservative Presbyterians in the mainline Presbyterian churches of the twentieth century.[7] The unfaithfulness of many denominations and even the persecution of faithful officers within those denominations corrupted the wholesome purposes of biblical church government. Many Christians looked outside denominational structures for fellowship, evangelism, and missions. The result was an unfortunate distancing of church government and the biblical mandate of evangelism and discipleship.

This course of events did little to stem the tide of individualism and self-sufficiency that have long characterized American Christianity.[8] American evangelicals often exhibit distrust of institutions and authority, including that of the church. Such patterns run against the grain of the Bible's teaching on the church. The Scripture tells believers that we need one another, and particularly the faithful labors of the officers of the church, in order to grow in the Christian life (see Eph. 4:11–16).

Perhaps one step toward a recovery of interest in church polity in the contemporary Presbyterian church is to consider why the doctrine

6. See for instance Robert C. Cannada and W. Jack Williamson, *The Historic Polity of the PCA* (Greenville, SC: A Press, 1997).

7. These have been chronicled in such works as Morton Smith, *How Is the Gold Become Dim: The Decline of the Presbyterian Church, U.S., as Reflected in Its Assembly Actions,* 2nd ed. (Jackson, MS: Steering Committee for a Continuing Presbyterian Church, 1973); John Edwards Richards, *The Historical Birth of the Presbyterian Church in America* (Liberty Hill, SC: Liberty Press, 1987).

8. See particularly Nathan Hatch, *The Democratization of American Christianity* (New Haven, CT: Yale University Press, 1989).

of the church might have been so important to our Presbyterian forefathers. Because they were wholeheartedly committed to the Bible, we may fairly surmise that their concern and labors reflected biblical priorities. In fact, we may consider four ways in which the Scriptures stress the importance of the church.

First, there is a close biblical connection between Christ and his church. Christ is the head of his body, the church (Col. 1:18, 24; Eph. 5:23; Acts 9:5). Christ's interests are bound up with the church. To study and to honor the government of the church is to bring glory to Jesus who has instituted that government for his own glory and for his church's good. One reason, for instance, that Reformed Protestants so vigorously protested the Pope's claim to be the vicar of Christ on earth is that they understood this claim to usurp Christ's exclusive right to rule the church.

Second, the church is a body that is both divinely created and divinely ruled. The church is divinely created. She is not a mere voluntary association of persons with similar interests, backgrounds, or goals. In this respect, she is different from the Kiwanis or the Junior League. Adults enter the church when they profess themselves to be "sinners in the sight of God, justly deserving His displeasure, and without hope save in his sovereign mercy." They profess to "believe in the Lord Jesus Christ as the Son of God, and Savior of sinners, and [to] receive and rest upon Him alone for salvation as He is offered in the Gospel."[9] The taking of such vows is to "enter into a solemn covenant with God and His Church."[10]

The church is also divinely ruled. The church is the body of Christ, who is the only head of the church. Part of what it means for Jesus to be the head of the church is that he has an exclusive and unique claim of authority upon the church. The Old Testament taught believers of old to expect God himself to come and to reign over his people (see Psalms 2, 110). The New Testament frequently quotes these psalms as

---

9. These statements have been drawn from the membership vows of the Presbyterian Church in America. See *BCO* 57–5. The vows of membership used by other Presbyterian and Reformed bodies address similar concerns as those broached here.

10. *BCO* 57–5.

finding their fulfillment in the person and work of Jesus Christ.[11] This is one of the many ways in which the New Testament shows us that Jesus is King over his people. Jesus is no absentee ruler. He is actively, intimately, and presently involved in ruling his church. One important way that Jesus rules his people is through the government that he has instituted in his Word.

Third, the church is the visible representation of the reign of Christ on earth. This is what the Westminster Confession of Faith means when it identifies the "visible Church" with "the kingdom of the Lord Jesus Christ" (WCF 25.2). Without getting into the question of the precise relationship between the Kingdom of God and the visible church, we may simply note that the Confession, following the Scripture, identifies the church as the place where Jesus' reign is now on particular display.[12] Seen in this light, the government of the church takes on pointed significance. Church polity is a way to give concrete and visible expression to the present reign of our risen and exalted Mediator, Jesus Christ.

Fourth, Jesus has uniquely tasked the church with the work of missions. Our Presbyterian forefathers debated whether organizations outside the church (parachurch organizations) should undertake the work of the Great Commission.[13] There was no disagreement, however, that Jesus had particularly called the church to bear the gospel to the nations.

The Great Commission of Jesus to his disciples in Matthew 28:18–20 is instructive. Jesus appears to his disciples after his resurrec-

11. The most recent edition of the Greek New Testament from United Bible Societies (UBS) lists citations of Ps. 2 at Acts 4:25–26 (Ps. 2:1); Acts 13:33; Heb. 1:5; 5:5 (Ps. 2:7); and citations of Ps. 110 at Matt. 22:44 and parallels; Matt. 26:64 and parallels; Acts 2:34–35; Heb. 1:13 (Ps. 110:1); Heb. 5:6; 7:17, 21 (Ps. 110:4). See *The Greek New Testament*, 4th rev. ed., ed. Barbara Aland et al. (Stuttgart: Deutsche Bibelgesellschaft/United Bible Societies, 1983), 887–88. See also the much more extensive list of "allusions and verbal parallels" at 895–96.

12. On the relationship between the church and the kingdom, see Geerhardus Vos, *The Teaching of Jesus concerning the Kingdom and the Church* (1903; repr. Nutley, NJ: Presbyterian and Reformed, 1972).

13. For nineteenth-century arguments upholding the unique role of the church as the missionary agency of Christ, see Thornwell, *Collected Writings*, 4:143–295; Benjamin M. Palmer, "Lay Evangelism and the Young Man's Christian Associations," *Southern Presbyterian Review* 29, 2 (April 1878): 354–77; Robert L. Dabney, "Lay Preaching," *Southern Presbyterian Review* 27, 2 (April 1876): 228–49; repr. in Dabney, *Discussions*, 2:76–95.

tion, telling them, "All authority in heaven and on earth has been given to me" (28:18). Jesus is referring, of course, to the authority that the Father had granted him, as Messiah, upon his resurrection. In view of that authority, he gives a commission to "the eleven disciples" (28:16). The commission may have application to the church generally, but the commission belongs particularly to the disciples, and to all those who after them were called to bring the Word of God to the nations. In other words, this commission has primary application to the ministers of the church.

The disciples must "go and make disciples of all nations, baptizing them in the name of the Father and of the Son and of the Holy Spirit, teaching them to observe all that I have commanded you" (28:19–20a). The disciples are to go to the nations and to make disciples of them.[14] In other words, they are God's means of bringing the nations into glad submission to the saving reign of Christ, to bring men and women alongside them as disciples of the Lord Jesus.

By what means will Christ's ministers make disciples of the nations?[15] Christ provides two means in this commission. Christ's ministers will baptize them in the triune name of God (28:19), and they will teach them all that Christ has taught his church through his apostles (28:20). The Great Commission does not end when a person makes public profession of faith and is baptized. Rather, the Great Commission has just begun. Jesus likens the church to a school where his disciples are continuously taught from the Word of God. The New Testament goes on to tell us that disciples are "taught to observe all that [Jesus] has commanded" them

14. The English word *go* translates the aorist participle *poreuthentes*, while the English words *make disciples* translate the aorist imperative *matheteusate*. Daniel Wallace has noted that "in Matthew . . . every other instance of the aorist participle of *poreuomai* followed by an aorist main verb (either indicative or imperative) is clearly attendant circumstance" (*Greek Grammar beyond the Basics: An Exegetical Syntax of the New Testament* [Grand Rapids: Zondervan, 1996], 645). The participle *poreuthentes* ("go") is best understood, then, as an attendant circumstance participle. Therefore, it should not be treated as an imperative coordinate with the imperative translated "make disciples." See here the caution voiced by R. T. France, *The Gospel according to Matthew,* NICNT (Grand Rapids: Eerdmans, 2007), 1115n34.

15. The participles *baptizontes* and *didaskontes* (Matt. 28:19, 20) are likely participles of means. See Wallace, *Greek Grammar,* 645; France, *The Gospel according to Matthew,* 1115.

through the preaching of the Word of God and through the discipline of the church (see 2 Tim. 4:1–5 and 1 Cor. 5:1–13, respectively).

What does all this have to do with the government of the church? Put simply, for the church to carry out the Great Commission faithfully, she must be governed well. The ministry of the Word through the officers of the church, and the discipline of the church are matters relating to the government of the church. The integrity of the church's missionary calling, then, is bound up with the polity of the church.

This pattern is precisely what we see in the book of Acts. The example of Paul, Barnabas, and the church at Antioch is especially instructive. In Acts, the church commissions and sends out Paul and Barnabas to preach the gospel (Acts 13:1–3). These men had been gifted and called by the Spirit to a particular work (Acts 13:2). The church recognizes that God has called them and therefore sets them apart by the laying on of hands (Acts 13:3). The church then sends them out to the work God has called them to do (Acts 13:3).

These two missionaries preach the gospel and then organize those who profess faith as local congregations: "And when they had appointed elders for them in every church, with prayer and fasting they committed them to the Lord in whom they believed" (Acts 14:23). Paul and Barnabas then return to their sending church for mutual encouragement (Acts 14:26–28), and subsequently return to the newly planted churches for ongoing encouragement and instruction: "Let us return and visit the brothers in every city where we proclaimed the word of the Lord, and see how they are" (Acts 15:36). Before Paul sets off on this next missionary journey, he participates in a spirited ecclesiastical assembly in Jerusalem (see Acts 15:1–35). The fruit of this meeting is a decree that, among other things, formally reaffirms the church's commitment to the gospel that she is proclaiming to the nations (see Acts 15:22–35).

In short, properly functioning church government is critical to the church's faithfulness as the missionary agency which Christ has appointed on earth.

Our Presbyterian forefathers valued the government of the church because they understood the importance and place of church polity within the Scriptures' teaching on the life of the church and on the life of the Christian. They understood that faithfulness to the pattern of the church's government set forth in the Scriptures was nothing less than faithfulness to Christ himself. Because they grasped the biblical relationship between the government of the church and the reign of their exalted Savior and Lord, their love for the Savior drove them to give careful attention to the workings of the church. It is my hope that this same love for Christ may drive us, as the church, to prize and to commit ourselves afresh to the government that Christ has given to us.

AND YET . . .

Since I have stressed the importance of the church and of church government, it might be helpful to make a couple of comments to avoid misunderstanding.

First, I am not saying that non-Presbyterian churches are not true churches because they are not Presbyterian. To use a classic distinction, biblical church government is crucial to the well-being (*bene esse*) but not to the existence (*esse*) of the church. In the words of the *Book of Church Order* of the PCA, "This scriptural doctrine of Presbytery is necessary to the perfection of the order of the visible Church, but is not essential to its existence."[16] We therefore embrace as brothers and co-laborers in Christ those believers who differ with us on matters of church government. We acknowledge that their church membership and credentials as officers are valid.[17] It is our hope, however, that brothers who differ with us and who read this book will, in true Berean spirit, weigh our arguments in light of the Scripture.

Second, I am not saying that Presbyterian government is itself the source of life in the church. It is the Spirit of Christ who brings the dead to life, and who strengthens and empowers the disciples of Christ for his service. F. P. Ramsay, an important nineteenth-century commentator on

16. *BCO* 1–7.
17. Morton Smith, *Commentary on the Book of Church Order of the Presbyterian Church in America*, 6th ed. (Taylors, SC: Presbyterian Press, 2007), 31.

the polity of the Presbyterian Church in the United States, powerfully presses this point.

> The church is a spiritual organization. . . . It must do all *its doings* in the Spirit. It is not constitutional regularity, it is not mechanical perfection, that makes the church efficient for its end; it is the Spirit of Christ using the church as his agent. . . . Alas, form and machinery may exist without life and power.[18]

Ramsay goes on to say, "This Spirit creates fit instruments for his own use, and therefore we may expect the church to become more nearly perfect in organization and methods as it becomes more perfectly the obedient organ of the Holy Spirit."[19] To be sure, the Spirit and not church government is the source of the church's life and power. And yet, God works by means. The government of the church is one of those appointed means. If we long to see the church prosper and flourish, we cannot both look to that hope and at the same time neglect the church's government.

WHAT THIS BOOK IS—AND IS NOT

What is this book supposed to be? This work makes no claim to give exhaustive treatments of the full range of the topics of Presbyterian polity. It will not try to give the definitive word on some of the nagging questions relating to church polity that have been with the church for decades, even centuries. Neither does it try to offer thorough rebuttals of such other forms of church government as episcopacy and congregationalism. Nor is this work an extensive commentary on the *Book of Church Order* of the PCA or on the forms of government of other Presbyterian bodies. The book is not intended exclusively for members and officers of the PCA. While the author is part of the PCA, my goal is

18. F. P. Ramsay, *An Exposition of the Form of Government and the Rules of Discipline of the Presbyterian Church in the United States* (Richmond, VA: Presbyterian Committee of Publication, 1898), 9–10.
19. Ibid., 10.

that non-PCA Presbyterians would learn from this work and apply what they learn from the Scriptures in their own denominational settings.

This book, rather, intends to accomplish two related goals. It offers a biblical case for the Presbyterian form of church government. I believe that the government that Christ has appointed for his church is Presbyterian in nature, and that the Scriptures bear out this fact. In saying this, I want to be clear that I do not believe that every (or even most) of the details of, say, the *Book of Church Order* are explicitly taught in some passage of Scripture or another. As we shall argue, this claim itself is rooted in biblical teaching.

In making this case, I make no claim to originality or ingenuity. I stand on the shoulders of giants. My debt to older writers on the subject of church government will be everywhere evident. My desire is to give classic arguments their biblical expression for a contemporary audience. If I am able to articulate Presbyterianism from the Scriptures to the church at the dawn of the twenty-first century, then I have accomplished what I have set out to do.

My second goal is to make this case as accessible as possible. I have above urged that knowledge of the church's government is beneficial not only to the officers of the church, but also to each of her members. I realize that ministers, elders, and seminary students have particular interest in the government of the church. My desire in writing this book, however, is that members and officers, Presbyterians and non-Presbyterians alike would read, study, consider, and weigh its contents.

For those who come to the Presbyterian church from a non-Presbyterian background, church polity can be something of a puzzle. This was certainly true to my own experience as a non-Presbyterian new believer coming to Presbyterianism. What's more, there are few contemporary resources available that lay out the biblical foundations of Presbyterian polity. I have intended this book to be just such a resource.

I am privileged to serve on the faculty of Reformed Theological Seminary, Jackson, and to teach church polity to seminary students each year. I hold membership, as a minister, in a PCA presbytery and am given opportunities to serve the church at many levels. I have witnessed

Presbyterian government work to my own spiritual good and to the good of the church that I am privileged to serve.

It is my hope that readers will see both the biblical truth and the practical implications of the Presbyterian form of government. I am not arguing that Presbyterianism is true because it works. I am arguing, rather, that Presbyterianism is true and that, by the blessing of Christ, it can and does work to his glory and to the good of his people. It is my hope and desire that this work may play some role, however small, to assist and to equip the people of God in serving our great and glorious Savior and King.

1

WHAT IS THE CHURCH?

Most Christians take it for granted that they should be active members of the local church. We can remember sermons that have helped us to understand Christian teaching, and have urged us to live faithfully for Christ. We can recall the spiritual help that the Lord's Supper and the prayers of the church have given us. We think of the fellowship that we have enjoyed with God's people—their encouragement and support in the hard times and in the good times.

This, of course, is no accident. Every Christian can testify to the many ways in which the church has been helpful to his or her Christian growth because God has designed the church and the Christian life to work together in just this way. In Colossians 2:19, the apostle Paul tells us that the church is like a human body with "joints and ligaments." Christians are bound together like the joints and sinews of the human body. It is "through the body's joints and ligaments," Paul says, that the "whole body" while "holding fast to the Head," that is Jesus, "grows with a growth that is from God."

The church is not only crucial to the Christian life but it is also crucial to God's redemptive plan and purpose, decreed from eternity and executed in history. There is, therefore, hardly a page of Scripture that does not, in some way, teach us about the church, or the people of God.

Before we look at the specifics of the government of the church, let us consider three interrelated lines of biblical teaching about the church. The first line to consider is the church in the history of redemption. In other words, what place do the people of God have in God's plan to redeem sinners by the work of his Son? The second line is an important distinction that the Scriptures use to discuss the people of God. This distinction has come to be known as the "visible" and "invisible" church. Because this distinction is both important and easily misunderstood, we want to give some thought to it. The third line is membership in the church. We will take up this biblical line of teaching by asking and answering two questions. First, is membership in the church necessary for Christians? Second, just who are the members of the church?

THE CHURCH IN REDEMPTIVE HISTORY

One People?

You may be wondering why I have been using the word "church" to describe the people of God in every age of redemptive history. Does the word "church" apply to Israel under the Old Testament? Perhaps you were under the impression that the church was born on the day of Pentecost (Acts 2).

When we examine the Scriptures, we find out that God has had a single people throughout the history of redemption. He did not replace Israel with an entirely new people, the church. Rather, to borrow the language of the Westminster Confession of Faith, the "people of Israel [was] a church under age" (19.3).

What is the biblical evidence that God has had a single people across redemptive history, frequently called "Israel" under the Old Testament, and "church" under the New Testament? How do we know that Israel and the church are the Old Covenant and New Covenant titles of God's one people, respectively? One passage that helps us is Romans 11, in which

2

Paul is dealing with a serious pastoral question. Does the fact that many Jews in Paul's day were rejecting the gospel mean that "God has rejected his people" (11:1)? Paul answers emphatically in the negative. He does so in two ways.[1] He urges, first, that Israel's fall is not total (11:1–10): "at the present time there is a remnant, chosen by grace" (11:5). Second, he reasons that Israel's fall is not final (11:11–32). He envisions the "full inclusion" of Israel (11:12). Specifically, "a partial hardening has come upon Israel until the fullness of the Gentiles has come in. And in this way all Israel will be saved" (11:25b–26a). Reformed commentators differ on exactly what Paul is envisioning in these verses, but Paul's basic point is clear.[2] God has not reneged on his commitments and promises. He is faithful and trustworthy.

Paul stresses that Israel's unbelief is not without purpose. By Israel's unbelief God is bringing salvation to the nations, for "through their trespass salvation has come to the Gentiles, so as to make Israel jealous." "Their trespass means riches for the world," "their failure means riches for the Gentiles," and "their rejection means the reconciliation of the world" (11:12, 15).

The apostle uses a striking picture to help us understand what he means. He compares the people of God to an olive tree at Romans 11:16b–24. Some of the "natural branches" were "broken off because of their unbelief" (11:21, 20). Here Paul is thinking about the unbelieving Jews. Those Jews who rejected Christ as he was offered to them in the gospel were cut off from the people of God. Other branches, Paul says, "were grafted in among the others and now share in the nourishing root of the olive tree" (11:17). Here Paul is thinking of Gentiles who, by the grace of God, have come to faith in Christ. They have been brought into the people of God. Notice how Paul summarizes his point at Romans 11:24: "For if you [Gentiles believers] were cut off from what is by nature a wild olive tree, and grafted, contrary to nature, into a cultivated olive

1. The following distinction comes from John Murray, *The Epistle to the Romans,* 2 vols., NICNT (Grand Rapids: Eerdmans, 1959, 1965), 2:75.

2. For a recent survey of opinion, see Douglas Moo, *The Epistle to the Romans,* NICNT (Grand Rapids: Eerdmans, 1996), 710–39.

tree, how much more will these, the natural branches, be grafted back into their own olive tree."

This passage has many things to say to Christians today. It encourages us to pray for the salvation of unbelieving Jews. It rebukes Christians who boast in their position in the church as they witness the "broken branches" (see 11:19–23).

In addition to these matters, Paul's picture in Romans 11 teaches us an important truth about the people of God: God has always had one people in redemptive history. There is one root that supports the branches (11:16b, 18). Certain branches are broken off, and "wild" branches are grafted in, but there is only one tree. To put it another way, in providence God has removed unbelieving Jews from his people and has included believing Gentiles within his people. He did not chop down one tree and plant another! God has always had a single people to call his own.

The epistle to the Hebrews gives us another picture to illustrate the same point.[3] After a breathtaking opening unfolding the splendor and majesty of the person and finished work of Jesus Christ (1:1–4), the author proceeds to argue for Christ's superiority. Jesus is superior to the angels (Heb. 1–2). In Hebrews 3–4, we learn that Jesus is superior to Joshua. In Hebrews 5–7, we learn that he is superior to the Levitical priests of the Old Testament era. In Hebrews 8–10, we learn that his work is superior to anything realized under the Old Covenant tabernacle and temple systems.

In Hebrews 3, the writer stresses that Jesus is superior to Moses.

> Therefore, holy brothers, you who share in a heavenly calling, consider Jesus, the apostle and high priest of our confession, who was faithful to him who appointed him, just as Moses also was faithful in all God's house. For Jesus has been counted worthy of more glory as the builder of a house has more honor than the house itself. (For every house is built by someone, but the builder of all things is God.) Now Moses

---

3. Hebrews does not claim to be written by any particular individual. For centuries, the church has been unable successfully to identify its author. For this reason, I will refer to him as "the writer" or "the author."

4

was faithful in all God's house as a servant, to testify to the things that were to be spoken later, but Christ is faithful over God's house as a son. And we are his house if indeed we hold fast our confidence and our boasting in our hope. (Heb. 3:1–6)

In saying that Jesus was "faithful to him who appointed him," the author does not suggest that Moses was unfaithful. On the contrary, he affirms that "Moses also was faithful in all God's house."

Even so, Jesus excels Moses. How is this the case? Jesus is "the builder of the house" (3:3). As such, he has more glory than the house itself and, by implication, than the servant of the house, Moses.[4] Further, while Moses "was faithful *in* all God's house as a servant" (3:5, emphasis mine), Jesus is "faithful *over* God's house as a son" (3:6, emphasis mine). Moses is the servant-in-the-house. Jesus is the son-over-the-house.

But what exactly is this house? The writer tells us in verse 6: "and we are his house if indeed we hold fast our confidence and our boasting in our hope." The house, in other words, is the people of God.

Notice that there is only one house in this passage. Moses served in this house, and Jesus stands over this house, but it is the same house. God has had one and only one people throughout redemptive history.

That God has one people throughout redemptive history helps us to understand some of the ways in which the New Testament writers address Christians. The apostle Peter, for instance, says of believers that they are "a chosen race, a royal priesthood, a holy nation, a people for his own possession" (1 Peter 2:9a). These are precisely the ways in which God addressed Israel in the Old Testament, as, for example, Exodus 19:5, 6: "you shall be my treasured possession among all peoples . . . and you shall be to me a kingdom of priests and a holy nation." The apostle Peter, furthermore, can greet the church in these terms: "to those who are elect exiles of the dispersion in Pontus, Galatia, Cappadocia,

4. In stating "the builder of all things is God" at verse 4, Hebrews once again affirms the deity of Jesus Christ.

Asia, and Bithynia" (1 Peter 1:1). Paul likely addresses the church as the "Israel of God" at Galatians 6:16.[5]

How is it that the apostles can speak this way? It is because the Scriptures understand there to be a single people of God across redemptive history. In light of that reality, the titles that the Old Testament ascribes to Israel can just as easily be ascribed to the church.

The Church in God's Plan

The Scriptures not only tell us that God has had a single people across redemptive history. They also tell us that the church has a crucial place in God's unfolding redemptive plan. We will not take the time to develop the point at length, but just as God has had one people in redemptive history, he has also had in redemptive history a single plan to redeem sinners.[6] One plan, one people. One purpose to redeem, one body of the redeemed.

This purpose to redeem was first announced in the Garden of Eden, after Adam sinned against God by eating the forbidden fruit from the tree of the knowledge of good and evil. God says to Adam and Eve, "I will put enmity between you and the woman, and between your offspring and her offspring; he shall bruise your head, and you shall bruise his heel" (Gen. 3:15). Many Christians have rightly seen this passage as *protoevangelium*, which is Latin for "the first announcement of the gospel." In dim and shadowy terms, God is announcing his plan to save sinners. He will do so by raising from Eve a descendant, whom the New

5. The verse reads, "And as for all who walk by this rule, peace and mercy be upon them, and upon the Israel of God." There is debate concerning whether Paul has in mind two groups, the church and ethnic Israel ("all who walk by this rule" and "the Israel of God") or a single group, the church ("all who walk by this rule," that is, "the Israel of God"). If Paul has in mind a single group, the church, then he has applied the title "Israel" to the church. Given that Paul has been throughout Galatians arguing that believers in every age are the children of Abraham, it is unlikely that he would conclude his epistle by "split[ting] up Jews and Gentles and includ[ing] only Jews under the privileged title the 'Israel of God.'" Michael F. Bird, *Introducing Paul* (Downers Grove: IL: InterVarsity, 2008), 50.

6. See O. Palmer Robertson, *The Christ of the Covenants* (Phillipsburg, NJ: Presbyterian and Reformed, 1980), and *Covenants: God's Way with His People* (Philadelphia: Great Commission Publications, 1987).

Testament tells us is Jesus Christ.[7] Although Satan would "bruise [Jesus'] heel" at the cross, Jesus would "bruise [Satan's] head" at the cross and in his resurrection. In other words, Jesus would deal Satan the mortal blow (see Rom. 16:20; Heb. 2:14–15).

The rest of the Old Testament is commentary on this verse. Who is this offspring? How will he come into the world? How will he defeat the devil and save God's people? One way that God develops this promise throughout the Old Testament is through a series of covenants that he makes with his people. His covenant with Noah, his covenant with Abraham, his covenant with Israel at Mount Sinai, his covenant with David, and the "New" Covenant prophesied by Jeremiah all tell us increasingly more about God's purpose to save sinners through Jesus, and bring us closer and closer to the arrival of Jesus, who would bring to fulfillment God's redemptive plan.

One of the things that we learn as we study the progress of God's plan to save sinners across redemptive history is that God was at work to do more than to save sinners individually. To be sure, God does save sinners individually. Each person must, for himself, repent and believe in Christ according to the gospel. To be a true Christian, he must be personally indwelt and empowered by the Spirit of Christ. It is in this sense that the saying is true, "God has children but he does not have grandchildren."

At the same time, God stresses throughout redemptive history that he is saving sinners as a body, as a multitude. As Stuart Robinson put it in his classic work *The Church of God an Essential Element of the Gospel*, "It is set forth as a distinguishing feature of the purpose of redemption, that it is to save not merely myriads of men as *individual men*, but myriads of sinners, as composing a Mediatorial body, of which the Mediator shall be the head."[8] In other words, the church-as-the-church is an indispensible part of God's plan to save sinners.

---

7. As Geerhardus Vos correctly observes, since the "serpent" in view is a single individual (the devil), we should understand the promised "offspring of the woman" in terms of a single descendant, *Biblical Theology: Old and New Testaments* (Edinburgh: Banner of Truth, 1975), 42.

8. Stuart Robinson, *The Church of God as an Essential Element of the Gospel* (Philadelphia: Joseph M. Wilson, 1858; repr., Willow Grove, PA), 34.

How do we see this in the Old Testament? We have already seen it in Genesis 3:15, the "first announcement of the gospel." God says here, "I will put enmity between you and the woman, and between your offspring and her offspring." We argued above that this verse is prophesying Jesus' victory over the devil. The verse is also saying something else. God is going to put a spiritual division within humanity. Some will be aligned spiritually with the devil. Others, by grace, will be aligned spiritually with God. We see this division and the conflict that results in Genesis 4, where we read of Cain slaying Abel. The apostle John comments on this grim event: "We should not be like Cain, who was of the evil one and murdered his brother. And why did he murder him? Because his own deeds were evil and his brother's righteous" (1 John 3:12). Cain was spiritually aligned with the devil, while Abel was spiritually aligned with God.[9]

After Abel was murdered, God raised up Seth in his place (Gen. 4:25). In the generation of Seth's son, Enosh, we read, "people began to call upon the name of the LORD" (Gen. 4:26). That is to say, people began to gather publically to worship the LORD.[10] God's promise to redeem sinners established a people who would be set apart from the world and who would offer him true, sincere worship.

The covenant that God makes with Noah (Gen. 6, 9) reflects the serious spiritual dangers in which the people of God found themselves. God judges the earth and delivers Noah and his family in view of the people of God's sinful intermarrying with unbelievers.[11] God institutes this covenant for the preservation and for the spiritual well-being of his people.[12]

---

9. We see this in Genesis, when Abel, in an act of worship, brings an offering to God. Moses comments, "And the LORD had regard for Abel and his offering, but for Cain and his offering he had no regard" (4:4b–5a). It is not just Abel's offering that the LORD regards, it is Abel himself.

10. Compare Ps. 116:17, where the psalmist says, "I will offer to you the sacrifice of thanksgiving and call on the name of the LORD." Since "call on the name of the LORD" is in parallel relationship with "offer[ing] the sacrifice of thanksgiving," and the latter is an act of worship, we may conclude that "to call on the name of the LORD" is an act of worship also.

11. That is, the "sons of God came in to the daughters of man and they bore children to them" (6:4). The "sons of God" likely refers to the people of God, and the "daughters of man" likely refers to the world of unbelievers.

12. See further Robertson, *Christ of the Covenants*, 109–25.

It is the covenant that God establishes with Abraham in Genesis 17, however, that preeminently illustrates the importance of the church to God's redemptive plan. In fact, Robinson has termed this covenant the "ecclesiological covenant" (that is, a covenant that fundamentally relates to the church).[13] In this covenant, the people of God are "visibly and formally set apart to become the special people of Messiah."[14] It is at this point in the history of redemption, Robinson observes, that "the promise of the Messiah, the Victor over Satan, takes the definite form of the Deliverer, Lawgiver, and Ruler of a people."[15]

Furthermore, this covenant anticipates God's plan to extend the gospel, through the promised offspring of Abraham, to the entire world (cf. Gen. 12:1–3). Circumcision, the sign of God's covenant, was at that time administered even to members of Abraham's household who were not physically descended from him (Gen. 17:12–13). In this small way, we catch a glimpse of God's purpose to establish a redeemed people from every nation, tribe, people, and language (Rev. 7:9).

As Robinson observes, the Abrahamic covenant sets the stage for the rest of the covenants of redemptive history.

> The covenant with Abraham is specifically with him, as representative and head of a separate society. The covenant made through Moses is with this society itself, now actually existing. The covenant with David stipulates for a King, who shall rule over this peculiar society as its perpetual head. And when, in the fullness of time, the King manifests himself, it is not claiming directly the headship of the world at large, but of a kingdom not of this world. His mission is to the lost sheep of the house of Israel, and to sit upon the throne of David.[16]

In other words, the Mosaic covenant (Exod. 19) orders the life of the society that God has brought forth from Abraham. God's covenant with David (2 Sam. 7) specifically promises that the people of God shall be

13. Robinson, *The Church of God*, 42.
14. Ibid., 43.
15. Ibid.
16. Ibid., 42.

ruled by a king descending from the line of David. The New Testament tells us that to Jesus "the LORD God will give . . . the throne of his father David" (Luke 1:32). Jesus is the one whom God had promised to David that he would "establish the throne of his kingdom forever" (2 Sam. 7:13).

Although Jesus rules the whole world as the Son of God, he exercises a special and distinct rule over his people as their Mediator and Head.[17] It is to this rule that Paul refers when he writes, "and he is head of the body, the church" (Col. 1:18). It is this rule that God's covenant with David envisioned. It is this rule of which the prophets so elegantly speak (see Isa. 9:1–7; 11:1–16; 33:17–24; Mic. 4:1–5; Ezek. 34).

The New Testament informs us that this people will be drawn not simply from ethnically Jewish persons. This people will be drawn from the "nations" to whom Jesus sends his disciples (Matt. 28:18–20). The apostle John shows us "a great multitude that no one could number, from every nation, from all tribes and peoples and languages standing before the throne and before the Lamb" in praise and adoration of Christ (Rev. 7:9). Surely in Jesus the blessing of Abraham has come to the nations (Gal. 3:14)!

The New Testament does not lose sight of the place that the church-as-the-church has in God's plan of redemption. We have already seen Paul relate the church to Christ as a human body to its head (Col. 2:19; see also Eph. 1:21–22; 5:23). In Matthew 28, we saw that Jesus reigns over his people as their king. And so Paul writes, "He has delivered us from the domain of darkness and transferred us to the kingdom of his beloved Son, in whom we have redemption, the forgiveness of sins" (Col. 1:13–14). Believers have exchanged the hard service of their former master, the devil, for the joyous service of King Jesus. The church, furthermore, is a family. We are the "household of God" (Eph. 2:19). As sons and daughters of the living God, every Christian is a brother to every other Christian.

What's more, the New Testament describes the people of God as the bride of Christ, their bridegroom (Mark 2:18–20; Eph. 5:22–33; 2 Cor. 11:2). Our great hope, as the people of God, is "the holy city,

---

17. Thus, we distinguish the "essential dominion" of God from the "mediatorial dominion" of Christ. We shall have more to say on this in the next chapter.

new Jerusalem, coming down out of heaven from God, prepared as a bride adorned for her husband" (Rev. 21:2). Redemptive history began with a promise of and to the church (Gen. 3:15). Fittingly, redemptive history closes with that promise wondrously fulfilled in Christ.

CHURCH "VISIBLE" AND "INVISIBLE"

It is at this juncture that we need to remind ourselves of another line of biblical teaching. This line has been described in terms of the "visible/invisible church" distinction. This is a longstanding distinction in Christian theology, and is expressed in chapter 25 of the Westminster Confession of Faith. The invisible church "consists of the whole number of the elect, that have been, are, or shall be gathered into one, under Christ the Head thereof; and is the spouse, the body, the fullness of Him that filleth all in all" (WCF 25.1).

The visible church, "which is also catholic or universal under the Gospel (not confined to one nation, as before under the law), consists of all those throughout the world that profess the true religion; and of their children; and is the kingdom of the Lord Jesus Christ, the house and family of God, out of which there is no ordinary possibility of salvation" (WCF 25.2).

It is important to recognize that the Westminster Standards are not claiming that the Scriptures teach that two churches exist, one invisible and one visible. They are not saying that the Christian must choose to which church he wishes to belong. Nor are they saying that the invisible church is "immaterial" while the visible church is "material."

How then are they different? First, the visible church is universal in nature. It is, however, the church as you and I see it in our generation. The invisible church, also universal, is spread across many generations. Second, one is a member of the visible church either by professing Christianity or by descending from a parent who professes Christianity. One is part of the invisible church by the eternal decree of God. Third, the numbers of the visible church increase or diminish. The numbers of the invisible church are fixed and never change.

11

Fourth and particularly important for our consideration, there are some members of the visible church who are not true members of the invisible church. One may profess faith insincerely and be reprobate, not elect. Furthermore, some members of the invisible church are not yet members of the visible church. Let us take up one example. Consider people who become genuine Christians later in life. Earlier in life, God had not yet regenerated them. We do not expect such persons at that point to have made profession of faith. When God does regenerate them, they will most certainly make profession of faith. For the time that they are unregenerate, however, we do not expect that these members of the invisible church will be part of the visible church.[18] Although they could not know it until they were regenerated and came to believe in Christ, as elect persons, they were all the while members of the invisible church.

Notice that the composition of the invisible church is fully known only to God. You, having made your calling and election sure, may be assured that you personally are part of the invisible church. You have no certain knowledge, however, of others who may be part of the invisible church. Of this body, "God alone judges with certainty concerning its members."[19]

The composition of the visible church, however, is based upon profession and descent. These are matters that you and I may see. These are matters that human beings can judge to be credible or not. Of this body, "man is also the judge."[20]

In summary, there is overlap but not identity between the visible church and invisible church. Those who profess and possess faith belong to the invisible and the visible church. Those who profess faith only and are reprobate belong to the visible church only. Persons who are elect but not yet regenerate belong to the invisible church but not yet to the visible church.

Where do we see this distinction reflected in the Scriptures? The apostle Paul recognizes this distinction within Israel. In Romans 2:28–29,

18. Unless, of course, they happen to descend from a parent who professes Christianity.
19. Thomas E. Peck, *Notes on Ecclesiology* (Richmond, VA: Presbyterian Committee of Publication, 1892; repr., Greenville, SC: Presbyterian Press, 2005), 16.
20. Ibid.

he says that it is possible to be a physically circumcised Jew, and yet not a true member of God's people: "For no one is a Jew who is merely one outwardly, nor is circumcision outward and physical. But a Jew is one inwardly, and circumcision is a matter of the heart, by the Spirit, not by the letter. His praise is not from man but from God."

Paul is not disparaging circumcision. He is not saying that it is bad to be circumcised. In fact, later in Romans Paul says that ethnic Israel enjoyed great privileges (Rom. 9:1–5). What Paul is saying is that one may be physically circumcised without being spiritually circumcised. In other words, one may have a mark on the flesh that we call circumcision. But he might not have a heart made new by the gracious working of the Spirit of God. There are Israelites, Paul says, and then there are *Israelites*. There are those who have only the sign of the covenant. And then there are those who have both the sign and the saving or redemptive benefits of the covenant. What Paul has described here is what the visible/invisible church distinction expresses.

Or consider Paul's argument later in Romans 9:6–18, where he applies this distinction to the history of the Old Covenant people of God, Israel. In Romans 9:6, he declares, "Not all who are descended from Israel belong to Israel." He remembers from Genesis that the promised offspring will be reckoned through Isaac not Ishmael: "it is not the children of the flesh who are the children of God, but the children of the promise are counted as offspring" (Rom. 9:8). God's true people, Paul goes on to argue, are not determined by biological descent or human activity. All that counts is the sovereign choice of God: "So then it depends not on human will or exertion, but on God who has mercy . . . he has mercy on whomever he wills, and he hardens whomever he wills" (Rom. 9:16, 18). Under the Old Covenant, then, there were two ways to reckon Israel. There were those whose claim to be Israelites was based only upon physical descent. True Israelites, however, while numbered among the visible people of God under the Old Covenant, were chosen and saved by a sovereign and merciful God. Once again, the visible/invisible church distinction expresses this biblical reality.

The visible/invisible church distinction is therefore biblical. But why is this important? It is so for at least two reasons. First, this distinction helps us to understand apostasy, that is, a person turning away from the faith that he or she once professed. Perhaps this is something that you have witnessed for yourself. A person gives every appearance of being a zealous Christian. He is in the pew every Sunday morning and Sunday evening. He is knowledgeable in the Scriptures. He seems to radiate the peace, joy, and love that belong to God's children. And then one day, he turns his back on Christ and his church. It is almost as if he has become a different person.

What are we to make of such persons? The Scriptures teach that no true child of God can ever completely or finally fall away from the state of grace.[21] Jesus says that of all whom the Father gives him, he will lose none, and he will raise them up on the last day (John 6:39). Believers, Peter says, are "by God's power being guarded through faith for a salvation ready to be revealed in the last time" (1 Peter 1:5). The Scriptures assure us that "he who began a good work in you will bring it to completion at the day of Christ Jesus" (Phil. 1:6).

At the same time, Scripture also teaches that sometimes persons profess faith when they do not possess faith. An example is Simon, described in Acts 8. When Philip preached the gospel in Samaria, the Bible says that "even Simon himself believed" and "after being baptized he continued with Philip" (Acts 8:13). Simon, however, later asked the apostles if he could purchase from them the ability to give the Holy Spirit (Acts 8:19–20). Peter gives Simon a stern rebuke (Acts 8:21–23). After telling him to repent, Peter says that Simon is "in the gall of bitterness and in the bond of iniquity" (Acts 8:23). What the Bible is saying is that Simon made a profession of faith even though his heart had been unchanged by the grace of God. For Simon, it was only a matter of time before his true character made itself known to those around him.

21. See here the summary of biblical teaching at WCF 17 and WLC 79. See the helpful treatment of Robert Peterson, *Our Secure Salvation: Perseverance and Apostasy* (Phillipsburg, NJ: P&R Publishing, 2009).

When we see people turning away from Christ and the church, we do not know what will happen to them in the future. It may be that they will repent and return to fellowship with God's people. It may be that they will continue in their rejection of Christ. In either case, we can be sure that no true child of God will ever completely or finally fall away. If they are true Christians, then God will restore them. If they are not, it may be that God will convert them. Or it may be that God will leave them in their sins. Here, the visible/invisible church distinction helps us to understand both the Bible's teaching on the perseverance of the saints and the Bible's recognition that sometimes members of the visible church reject the faith they once professed.

This distinction is important in a second way. It gives background to the way in which God calls the church to receive adult persons into her membership. The church judges a person's Christianity on the basis of what he or she professes to believe and the life that he or she is living. On that basis the church admits a person into its membership. In Presbyterian circles, this is sometimes called a "credible profession of faith." By "profession" we mean "an intelligent *profession* of true spiritual faith in Christ, which is not contradicted by the life." By "credible" we mean "that which can be believed to be genuine" not "that which convinces." It is "not a positive judging of his conversion, but determining negatively that there's no reason for pronouncing him not to be a Christian."[22] At no point has the church had infallible knowledge of the hearts of those seeking membership. This is a knowledge that God has not given to us.

Therefore the church, by design, is not a society of exclusively regenerate persons. It is our hope and prayer that the church will be pure, her members renewed by the grace of God. Membership in the church, however, is reckoned by profession not regeneration. This fact is good for every Christian to know. Church membership is not a declaration that I am a regenerate person. It is, rather, a declaration that the faith that I profess and the life that I live are credible or believable.

22. Archibald Alexander Hodge, *Outlines of Theology* (1879; Edinburgh: Banner of Truth, 1972), 645–46.

It is not an infallible assurance that I am a Christian. It is an assurance that fellow Christians regard me as a Christian.

MEMBERSHIP IN THE CHURCH

We are now ready to take up a third line of biblical teaching, that of membership in the church. We have two questions before us. First, is church membership necessary? Does a Christian *have* to be a member of the church? Second, what is the biblical definition of a member of the church? Whom does Scripture say may be admitted to the membership of the church?

Is Church Membership Necessary?

Is it necessary to join the church? We have seen above that the Christian draws great benefit from the service and fellowship of his fellow Christians. We have seen that the Scripture envisions the believer as one part of a much larger body, joined to its directing head, Jesus (Eph. 4:11–16; Col. 2:19). It is certainly profitable to join the church. But is it necessary?

Some Christians today challenge the necessity of church membership. On occasion this is done in theory. Some have reasoned, "I am a member of the invisible church, why then do I need to join the visible church? Surely membership in the visible church is redundant."

More often, however, this is seen in practice, when people simply fail to join the church. They may attend services, Bible studies, and participate in church-sponsored activities, but they are not recognized members of that body. They do not see the importance of joining the church and so do not take steps toward church membership. Compounding the problem is that there are certain congregations in the United States that neither require nor have church membership. One might say, "If these churches do not require me to join them, then why should I join the church?"

Situations like these send us to the Scriptures. Does the Bible require church membership? If so, why does it obligate Christians to join the church?[23]

23. Throughout this discussion we will be speaking of the individual Christian's relationship to the local congregation. Of course, when believers join the church, they are not merely

Scripture does in fact require church membership of believers.[24] If we look for a single verse that says "you must join the church," we will be disappointed. Rather, Scripture shows us the necessity of church membership in a different way. In showing us what the Christian life is, and what the church is, it leads us inescapably to the conclusion that Christians must join the church.

We see this conclusion in at least six ways. First, remember the Great Commission, which we discussed in the Introduction. Jesus commissions his disciples to "go and make disciples" of the nations. They are to do this in two ways. They are to baptize them, and they are to teach them everything that Jesus had commanded them to teach others. The Great Commission, we saw, does not end at conversion. It is just beginning at conversion. The Great Commission consists of both the ingathering *and* the perfecting of the saints.

But how is the Great Commission to be executed? The book of Acts gives us an answer to this question. In the Introduction, we observed a certain pattern to the work of missions from Acts, in which the Word is preached by men who are gifted and called by the Spirit, and sent out by the church. When the Holy Spirit blesses the preaching of the Word, men and women respond in faith and repentance. They then begin a common life together. In Acts 2:42, we read that the early disciples "devoted themselves to the apostles' teaching," and also shared a common life together (Acts 2:46). Luke comments that "the Lord added to their number day by day those who were being saved" (2:47). In other words, when a person professes faith in Christ, he is "added to" the existing body of believers. That is to say, he joins the church.

This is the pattern that we see again and again in Acts. The Word is preached, people profess faith, and they gather locally into congregations

---

part of that local body. They are members of the whole body of believers. See further our discussion in chapter 5.

24. For a helpful and thorough treatment of this subject, see the unpublished paper by Mark Herzer, "The Church: A Covenant Community." At the time of writing, this paper is available online. See also Wayne Mack, *To Be or Not to Be a Church Member? That Is the Question!* (Amityville, NY: Calvary, 2004); Wayne A. Mack and Dave Swavely, *Life in the Father's House: A Member's Guide to the Local Church,* rev. and exp. ed. (Phillipsburg, NJ: P&R Publishing, 2006), esp. pages 15–52.

or assemblies ruled by Christ through a government of his appointment (Acts 14:23). Their lives, individually and corporately, are governed by Christ through the Scriptures. There is no occasion in the Acts of the Apostles when an individual Christian lives a solitary existence, isolated from other believers. Christians, by definition, join themselves to the body of believers.

Second, many commands given to Christians in the New Testament assume church membership. Let us look at two examples. The New Testament commands believers to give due submission to church leaders. In 1 Thessalonians 5:12–13, Paul says, "We ask you, brothers, to respect those who labor among you and are over you in the Lord and admonish you, and to esteem them very highly in love because of their work." This command assumes that the Thessalonian believers had an acknowledged relationship with leaders in that church. Their leaders are "over them," are called to "admonish" them when necessary, and should receive the "respect" and "esteem" of those whom they serve. How did this relationship come into existence? It came into existence when the Thessalonian believers committed themselves to join the church at Thessalonica.

Or, consider Paul's exhortation at Colossians 3:13: "bearing with one another and, if one has a complaint against another, forgiving each other; as the Lord has forgiven you, so you also must forgive"; or at Colossians 3:16, "Let the word of Christ dwell in you richly, teaching and admonishing one another in all wisdom, singing psalms and hymns and spiritual songs, with thankfulness in your hearts to God." Christians have defined obligations to "one another." Whom does Paul have in mind when he says "one another"? The answer is found in the greeting of the letter: "to the saints and faithful brothers in Christ at Colossae" (Col. 1:2). The "one another" is the church at Colossae. Paul has in mind a specific and defined body of believers who have certain commitments and obligations to one another in that body. It is church membership that makes possible and gives rise to these commitments and obligations. Paul simply does not envision, here or anywhere else, free-floating Christians flitting from one congregation to the next. He assumes that Christians exist in the committed relationships that church membership solemnizes.

Third, Jesus' teaching about discipline in the church assumes the necessity of church membership. He tells his disciples at Matthew 18:17b of an unrepentant sinner, "and if he refuses to listen even to the church, let him be to you as a Gentile and a tax collector." By Christ's commandment, a person who persists in his sins should be confronted about his persistence in sin. If he remains impenitent, the one to confront him is the "church," that is, the assembly of the elders of the church.[25] If a person is not a member of the church, if he has no formal relationship with the church, then on what basis can the "church" confront him about his sin? The discipline of the church assumes church membership.

Paul makes the same point in his first epistle to the Corinthians. At 1 Corinthians 5, Paul addresses a church which has failed to confront one of its own about a serious, scandalous, and persistent sin. What does Paul tell the church to do? "Let him who has done this be removed from among you" (1 Cor. 5:2). This is to be done when the church is "assembled in the name of the Lord Jesus" and "with the power of our Lord Jesus" (1 Cor. 5:4). The aim or goal of discipline is not punitive but restorative: "you are to deliver this man to Satan for the destruction of the flesh, so that his spirit may be saved in the day of the Lord" (1 Cor. 5:5). Once again, this exercise of church discipline would be incomprehensible if the offending party were not a member of the church. He could not be "removed" from the church were he not already in the membership of the church.

Fourth, the sacrament of the Lord's Supper assumes the existence of church membership. Paul, again writing to the Corinthians, makes it clear that not everyone is entitled or permitted to come to the Lord's Table and so partake of the sacrament (1 Cor. 11:17–34). He gives

---

25. By *church*, Jesus does not refer to the congregation as such. He means, rather, the assembly of the elders. We will return to this point more fully in chapter 3. In light of these considerations, T. David Gordon has helpfully suggested translating the Greek word *ekklesia* at Matthew 18:17 as "assembly," rather than "church." See his unpublished paper "When 'Church' is a Judicial Assembly."

specific directions to the church as to how the Lord's Supper is to be observed. He warns persons against "eating the bread or drinking the cup of the Lord in an unworthy manner" (1 Cor. 11:27). Each person must "examine himself . . . and so eat of the bread and drink of the cup" lest he bring "judgment on himself" (1 Cor. 11:28–29).

Notice the assumptions behind Paul's argument. Paul assumes that the Lord's Supper will be administered only in the church, when the church gathers for public worship (see Acts 20:7). He also assumes that those who approach the Lord's Table are professing Christians. This is what Paul has already stated at 1 Corinthians 10:16–17, namely, the Lord's Supper signifies the union of believers with Christ, and the unity of the body of believers.[26] But how is a person to be recognized as such a person in union and communion with Christ and in fellowship with other believers? The biblical pattern, we have seen, is that they formally join the church. This attachment to the church—church membership—is precisely what is assumed in the church's observance of the Lord's Supper. Without church membership, that which the Lord's Supper signifies (the fellowship of believers) would be, on biblical terms, meaningless.

Fifth, the passages discussing Christian growth that we considered above (Eph. 4:11–16, Col. 2:19) require church membership. The growth of the body, Paul says, requires "each part . . . working properly" (Eph. 4:16). Further, believers are joined to one another in the way that the parts of the human body are joined to one another. It is not simply that believers share in one another's gifts and graces. It is that they do so committed and bound to one another. How does this commitment and binding come to expression in the church? Church membership.

Sixth, the responsibility of the elders of the church requires church membership. At Hebrews 13:17a we read the following command, "Obey your leaders and submit to them, for they are keeping watch over your souls, as those who will give an account." The church's elders, or "leaders," are those who have oversight over the

26. Herzer, "The Church," 6.

"souls" of the congregation and, at the judgment day, must "give an account" to Christ for those souls. But unless the elders are in a defined relationship with a specific group of Christians, how can they oversee them, much less give an account for them? Without church membership, the elders of the church would be unable to fulfill their God-assigned task.[27]

In conclusion, the New Testament requires church membership of every professing Christian. Church membership underlies the government, discipline, worship, and life of the church. One is not at liberty to claim membership in the invisible church without also joining the church visible. Christian discipleship requires that one become a member of the church.

Who Are the Members of the Church?

We have seen that it is necessary to be a member of the church. We have seen that one attaches himself to the church by profession of faith. One final question is to consider more precisely who the members of the visible church are.

Above we quoted the Westminster Confession of Faith's definition of the visible church, which mentions two groups of people. There are those who make credible professions of faith, and there are the children of those who have made credible professions of faith.

Few object to receiving into the membership of the church persons who are able to profess the Christian faith and to adorn that profession with godly living. Some have objected, however, to acknowledging the children of such persons as members of the church. This objection explains one difference between Presbyterians and Baptists. Both acknowledge one another as Christians. Historically, Presbyterians and Baptists have agreed theologically on far more than they have differed. They differ, however, concerning whether the children of professing believers, as such, are members of the church. Presbyterians say "yes," while Baptists say "no."

---

27. I am grateful to T. David Gordon for alerting me to this argument.

What is the biblical evidence that the children of professing believers are by birthright members of the church and entitled to the church's recognition of their membership? As with our study of the necessity of church membership above, the answer to this question will not be found in a single verse. We must look at Scripture's teaching and consider some implications that surely follow from that teaching.

We begin with the covenant that God made with Abraham in Genesis 17. God intended this covenant to confirm the promises he had made to Abraham in Genesis 12 (see Gen. 17:5–6). This covenant embraced Abraham and his children such that Abraham and his children were recognized as part of the visible people of God. On this basis, Abraham's male children were to receive the covenant sign of circumcision: "And I will establish my covenant between me and you and your offspring after you throughout their generations for an everlasting covenant, to be God to you and to your offspring after you" (Gen. 17:7), and "This is my covenant, which you shall keep, between me and you and your offspring after you: Every male among you shall be circumcised" (Gen. 17:10).

Further, the covenant that God made with Abraham is an evangelical covenant. That is to say, this covenant administers the promises of the gospel. This is Paul's reasoning in Galatians 3:8: "And the Scripture, foreseeing that God would justify the Gentiles by faith, preached the gospel beforehand to Abraham, saying 'In you shall all the nations be blessed.' " Paul quotes here the promise that God makes to Abraham in Genesis 12. He further describes God's declaration of this promise to Abraham as "preaching the gospel beforehand." It is this promise that God designed the covenant of Genesis 17 to administer.

Not only was the promise evangelical, but the sign of the Abrahamic covenant is evangelical also. This is evident from Paul's description of circumcision at Romans 4:11: "a seal of the righteousness that Abraham had by faith" (compare Rom. 4:1–5). In signifying justification by faith alone, circumcision served to point Abraham and his children to the promise by which he—and believers in every age—was saved.

God has not nullified this covenant. This covenant embraces New Testament believers. This is why Paul calls believers "Abraham's offspring," and "sons of Abraham [through faith]" at Galatians 3:29 and Galatians 3:7. Paul calls the blessings of the gospel that New Testament believers presently enjoy the "blessing of Abraham" (Gal. 3:14). It is as "Abraham's offspring" that we are "heirs according to promise" (Gal. 3:29).

But if the Abrahamic covenant continues, what of the covenant sign of circumcision? What has become of circumcision? Under the New Covenant, the Scriptures argue, baptism has replaced circumcision as sign and seal of the covenant of grace. This is what Paul argues at Colossians 2:11–12.

> In him you also were circumcised with a circumcision made without hands, by putting off the body of the flesh, by the circumcision of Christ, having been buried with him in baptism, in which you were also raised with him through faith in the powerful working of God, who raised him from the dead.

What is Paul saying here? He is saying that believers have been "circumcised" by the "circumcision of Christ." This is not physical circumcision. It is "made without hands." That is to say, it is a work of God. This circumcision Paul describes in terms of the "putting off the body of flesh." Here, Paul is saying that the believer has a new relationship with sin ("the body of flesh"). Sin no longer has dominion over the believer. It no longer sits in the driver's seat, determining the believer's thoughts, choices, and actions. This is why Paul can say that the "body of flesh" has been "put off" (compare Col. 3:9, "you have put off the old self with its practices"). This "putting off" or "circumcision" describes what took place at the believer's regeneration. Compare what we saw Paul say at Romans 2:29: "but a Jew is one inwardly, and circumcision is a matter of the heart, by the Spirit, not by the letter." God has made the believer, once alive to sin and dead to righteousness, now, in Christ, dead to sin and alive to righteousness.

But "circumcision" is not the only way that Paul can here describe this decisive change in the believer. He says that believers have been "buried with [Christ] in baptism" and "raised with him." So fully has God united believers with Jesus in his death that Paul can say that they were "buried with him." God has so united believers with Jesus in his resurrection that Paul can say that they were "raised with him."

But Paul says that believers have been "buried with [Christ] *in baptism*." Is Paul talking about water baptism here? No. Paul is not primarily thinking of physical baptism any more than he is thinking of physical circumcision in Colossians 2. "Baptism" is Paul's way of talking about the decisive change that God has wrought in believers such that they have a brand new relationship with sin and with righteousness: "in which you were also raised with him through faith in the powerful working of God, who raised him from the dead."

Just as spiritual circumcision once had its counterpart in physical circumcision, so we may infer that spiritual baptism now has its counterpart in water baptism. That is to say, circumcision once served as sign and seal of the regeneration of the Old Testament believer. Now, baptism serves as sign and seal of the regeneration of the New Testament believer. We have the same grace represented under different signs.

This is precisely what we see in the New Testament. Christ commissions his disciples to "baptize" those who respond in faith to the gospel (Matt. 28:18–20). Later in the New Testament, we see that after persons make public profession of faith, they are baptized (Acts 2:38 with Acts 2:41; 8:12; 16:14–15, 31–33). Circumcision is no longer required of God's people (see Acts 15). Baptism does the job now that circumcision did prior to the coming of Christ.

This observation brings us to our final point. The children of believers during the Old Testament were, by divine command, to receive the covenant sign of circumcision. In the same way, the children of believers during the New Testament are, by the same command, to receive the covenant sign of baptism. In both cases, they are entitled to the sign of the covenant because they are by birthright members of the church.

24

But do we have any indication that the New Testament recognizes the children of believers to be members of the church? We do. Notice what Paul says at Ephesians 6:1–3.

> Children, obey your parents in the Lord, for this is right. "Honor your father and mother" (this is the first commandment with a promise), "that it may go well with you and that you may live long in the land."

Which children does Paul address? He addresses the children of believers in the church at Ephesus. How does Paul address these children? He addresses them as among "the saints who are in Ephesus, and are faithful in Christ Jesus" (Eph. 1:1). That is to say, he addresses them as members of the congregation. Why does he call the members of the church at Ephesus "saints" or "holy ones"? Paul here is not saying that they are all inwardly holy. He is saying that they are, by calling, set apart from the world, and set apart for God.

Children, then, are members of the church and, as such, are called to pursue holiness. In Ephesians 6:1–3, Paul tells the children of the congregation how they ought to live in light of that calling. In Ephesians 6:4, Paul tells the fathers of these children to "bring them up in the discipline and instruction of the Lord." These children, in other words, are called to be students in the school of Christ, to be disciples of Jesus.

Consider what Paul argues at 1 Corinthians 7:14: "the unbelieving husband is made holy because of his wife, and the unbelieving wife is made holy because of your husband. Otherwise your children would be unclean, but as it is, they are holy." The children of at least one believer are "holy" not "unclean." In light of our conclusions from Paul's statements in Ephesians, we may say they are "holy" in precisely the way that Paul called them holy in Ephesians 1:1. They are, by calling, set apart from the world, and set apart for God.

One might object, "But Paul says that the unbelieving wife is made holy because of her husband. Are you saying that unbelieving spouses should join the church simply because they are married to a believer?" In reply, observe the concern that Paul addresses in this passage. His main concern is the ecclesiastical standing of the child of a spiritually mixed marriage. Which spouse—the unbelieving or believing—determines that child's standing? Paul replies that the child ought to be recognized as a member of the visible church because of his relationship with his believing parent. In what sense are unbelieving spouses "holy"? They are "holy" in the sense that they are the ones through whom these "holy" children have come into the world.[28]

One final set of passages showing the recognition of the membership of children in the church and their entitlement to the sacrament of baptism are the "household baptisms" of Acts. We read that Lydia "was baptized and her household as well" (Acts 16:15). The Philippian jailor "was baptized at once, he and all his family" (Acts 16:33).

This is precisely what we expect to see. In Genesis 17, we saw that professing believers and their households received the covenant sign to indicate their membership in the church. In these New Testament passages, we are seeing professing believers and their households also receive the covenant sign to indicate their membership in the church.

One might object that there are no children, much less infants, mentioned in either of these baptisms. We may reply that it is not necessary for the Scripture to tell us precisely who was or was not part of that household. The important point for what we are trying to show is that the "household" was baptized upon the profession of faith of the head of that household.

One might also object that in Acts 18:8 the Scriptures say that Crispus's "entire household" believed. Does that not imply that the members of the jailor's household and Lydia's household believed also? Not necessarily. Whether or not the household believed, they were entitled to the sign of baptism once the head of the household made profession of faith. They were entitled to that sign because they

28. Charles Hodge paraphrases Paul's statement in this way: "[T]he pagan husband, in virtue of his union with a Christian wife, although he remained a pagan, was sanctified; he assumed a new relation; he was set apart to the service of God, as the guardian of one of his chosen ones, and as the parent of children who, in virtue of their believing mother, were children of the covenant." Charles Hodge, *An Exposition of the First Epistle to the Corinthians* (New York: Robert Carter, 1860), 116.

were members of the church by virtue of their relationship with the person professing faith.

In summary, the Scriptures recognize the children of a believing parent to be, by virtue of that relationship, members of the church. In other words, these children have an acknowledged relationship with the church; they stand under its government; they have privileges and responsibilities attending that membership.[29]

In saying that these children are members of the church, we are not saying that they are regenerate or will certainly become regenerate. We would not say this of any member of the church, whether under the Old Covenant or under the New Covenant. We are saying that, as the children of believers, they are entitled to certain privileges and have certain responsibilities.[30] They are owed the prayers, instruction, and admonition of their fellow church members. What should these children be taught? They should be taught that they are sinners in the sight of God, that they justly deserve the punishment of God for their sins, and that they need the cleansing of Christ's blood and the renewing of the Holy Spirit. They should be taught Scripture's pattern of mind and life that is pleasing to the Lord. They should be taught to turn to Christ in faith and repentance, and to live lives pleasing to him.

We have surveyed Scripture's teaching on the importance of the church in redemptive history. We have considered the biblical "visible/invisible church" distinction. We have considered why membership in the visible church is necessary for Christians, and why the Scriptures consider the children of believers to be members of the church. We are now ready to take a closer look at the government of the church.

---

29. I owe this three-fold definition to David F. Coffin Jr.

30. There are certain privileges that they may not exercise until they demonstrate the maturity and spiritual qualifications that Scripture requires for those privileges. One such privilege, of course, is admission to the Lord's Table (1 Cor. 11).

2

THE GOVERNMENT OF THE CHURCH

I n the last chapter, we saw that God has one people throughout the history of redemption. Since God first proclaimed the gospel to Adam and Eve, there has been one company comprised of those who profess the true religion, along with their children.

We have also seen that the church stands at the center of God's unfolding plan of redemption. This is true in Genesis, in Revelation, and at every point in between.

Why is it that the church has such an important place in God's unfolding redemptive purpose? The answer to this question is surely found in the church's relationship to her Savior and Head, Jesus Christ. In the Introduction, we observed the Bible's teaching that the visible church is the "kingdom of the Lord Jesus Christ" (WCF 25). The Scriptures point to the church as evidence of the glorious reign of Jesus over all things. The church uniquely puts on display the reign of Jesus to the world around her. In the church the world sees a body of persons professing submission to a majestic and risen King. When the Bible emphasizes the church in redemptive history it therefore places the spotlight on her King, Jesus.

To say that Jesus reigns over his church raises a number of questions. If the Bible teaches that God is sovereign over all that he has made, is it redundant to say that Jesus reigns over the church? Second, how can Jesus say to his disciples, "All authority in heaven and on earth *has been given to me*"? (Matt. 28:18). In other words, what does Jesus now have that he did not formerly possess? Further, since Jesus has ascended into heaven (Acts 1:9–10), by what means does he reign over his church dwelling on the earth? What relationship does Jesus' reign have to civil government? Do the Scriptures call the civil government to play any role in directing the affairs of the church? Do the Scriptures call church government to play any role in the affairs of the state?

These are all questions pertaining to the government of the church. In this chapter we will explore the Bible's teaching on the church's government by addressing these questions.

"JESUS SHALL REIGN WHERE'ER THE SUN DOTH ITS SUCCESSIVE JOURNEYS RUN"

The Bible is both clear and full in its teaching concerning the sovereignty of God. J. I. Packer has summarized this doctrine well.

> The assertion of God's absolute sovereignty in creation, providence, and grace is basic to biblical belief and biblical praise. The vision of God on the throne—that is, ruling—recurs. . . . We are constantly told in explicit terms that the Lord (Yahweh) reigns as king, exercising dominion over great and tiny things alike (Ex. 15:18; Ps. 47; 93; 96:10; 97; 99:1–5; 146:10; Prov. 16:33; 21:1; Is. 24:23; 52:7; Dan. 4:34–35; 5:21–28; 6:26; Matt. 10:29–31). God's dominion is total: he wills as he chooses, and carries out all that he wills, and none can stay his hand, or thwart his plans.[1]

The doctrine of divine sovereignty helps us to understand Scripture's teaching of the providence of God. God's works of providence, the Westminster Larger Catechism states, are "his most holy, wise, and powerful preserving and governing all his creatures; ordering them,

---

1. J. I. Packer, *Concise Theology: A Guide to Historic Christian Beliefs* (Wheaton, IL: Tyndale, 1993), 33.

and all their actions, to his own glory" (WLC 18). As Packer explains, "[By providence], the Creator, according to his own will, (a) keeps all creatures in being, (b) involves himself in all events, and (c) directs all things to their appointed end . . . God is completely in charge of his world. His hand may be hidden, but his rule is absolute."[2]

If the Bible affirms the sovereignty of the triune God in this way, how are we to make sense of Jesus' statement that "all authority in heaven and on earth *has been given to me*"? If Jesus is fully divine, and if the triune God is fully sovereign, then Jesus' sovereignty can neither increase nor diminish. So how then does Jesus speak of an authority that he has recently received?

Consider passages from the Old Testament that look ahead to the worldwide dominion of Jesus the Messiah:

> I saw in the night visions, and behold, with the clouds of heaven there came one like a son of man, and he came to the Ancient of Days and was presented before him. And to him was given dominion and glory and a kingdom, that all peoples, nations, and languages should serve him; his dominion is an everlasting dominion, which shall not pass away, and his kingdom one that shall not be destroyed. (Dan. 7:13–14)

> I will tell of the decree: The LORD said to me, "You are my Son; today I have begotten you. Ask of me, and I will make the nations your heritage, and the ends of the earth your possession." (Ps. 2:7–8)

> The LORD says to my Lord: "Sit at my right hand, until I make your enemies your footstool." The LORD sends forth from Zion your mighty scepter. Rule in the midst of your enemies! (Ps. 110:1–2)

> For unto us a child is born, to us a son is given; and the government shall be upon his shoulder, and his name shall be called Wonderful Counselor, Mighty God, Everlasting Father, Prince of Peace. Of the increase of his Government and of peace there will be no end, on the

2. Ibid., 54. See pages 54–55 for the dozens of biblical texts that Packer cites from Louis Berkhof's treatment of divine providence.

throne of David and over his kingdom, to establish it and to uphold it with justice and with righteousness from this time forth and forevermore. The zeal of the LORD of hosts will do this. (Isa. 9:6–7)

Consider passages from the New Testament that declare that Jesus, upon his resurrection and ascension, has assumed this worldwide, messianic reign:

For to this end Christ died and lived again, that he might be Lord both of the dead and of the living. (Rom. 14:9)

Then comes the end, when [Jesus] delivers the kingdom to God the Father after destroying every rule and every authority and power. For he must reign until he has put all his enemies under his feet. The last enemy to be destroyed is death. (1 Cor. 15:24–26)

And being found in human form, he humbled himself by becoming obedient to the point of death, even death on a cross. Therefore God has highly exalted him and bestowed on him the name that is above every name, so that at the name of Jesus every knee should bow in heaven and on earth and under the earth, and every tongue confess that Jesus Christ is Lord, to the glory of God the Father. (Phil. 2:8–11)

[The Father] raised [Jesus] from the dead and seated him at his right hand in the heavenly places, far above all rule and authority and power and dominion, and above every name that is named, not only in this age but also in the one to come. And he put all things under his feet and gave him as head over all things to the church, which is his body, the fullness of him who fills all in all. (Eph. 1:20–23)

Once again we may ask—how is it that Jesus assumed an authority and reign that he did not previously possess? The answer is found in an important distinction. We may distinguish Jesus' *essential* dominion or reign from his *mediatorial* dominion or reign. This is how Ebenezer Erskine and James Fisher, two eighteenth-century Scottish commentators on the Westminster Shorter Catechism, express the difference.

Q. 17. How *manifold* is [Jesus'] kingdom?

A. It is *twofold*; his *essential* and his *mediatorial* kingdom.

Q. 18. What is his *essential* kingdom?

A. It is that absolute and supreme power, which he hath over all the creatures in heaven and earth, *essentially* and *naturally*, as God equal with the Father, Psal. ciii. 19, "his kingdom ruleth over all—"

Q. 19. What is his *mediatorial* kingdom?

A. It is that sovereign power and authority in and over the *church*, which is given him as Mediator, Eph. i. 22.[3]

Jesus' essential reign belongs to him as Second Person of the Godhead. This reign is unchanging and unchangeable. Jesus' mediatorial reign, however, belongs to him as the Incarnate Son of God, the God-man. This reign he assumed upon his exaltation.[4] This reign is subject to change and may be said to increase or grow. This reign extends to the ends of the earth, but has the church as its particular focus. As the nineteenth-century American Presbyterian theologian Robert L. Dabney explained, "The Church is [Jesus'] immediate domain: its members are His citizens; and for their benefit His powers are all wielded. But His power extends over all the human race, the angelic ranks, good and bad, and the powers of nature."[5] In other words, in acknowledging Jesus' *essential* reign, believers particularly confess Jesus, with the Father and the Holy Spirit, to be God over all. In acknowledging Jesus' *mediatorial* reign, believers particularly confess Jesus to be the risen Lord who purchased them by his own blood.

3. James Fisher, *The Westminster Assembly's Shorter Catechism Explained by Way of Question and Answer*, 3rd ed. (repr., Philadelphia: Presbyterian Board of Christian Education, 1925), 138.

4. We should note, with A. A. Hodge, that "while Christ has been virtually mediatorial King as well as Prophet and Priest from the fall of Adam, yet his public and formal assumption of his throne and inauguration of his spiritual kingdom dates from his ascension and session at the right hand of his Father." Archibald Alexander Hodge, *Outlines of Theology* (1879; Edinburgh: Banner of Truth, 1972), 429.

5. Robert L. Dabney, *Systematic Theology*, 2nd ed. (St. Louis: Presbyterian Publishing Company of St. Louis, 1878; repr., Edinburgh: Banner of Truth, 1985), 550.

"AS PLANETS MOVING IN CONCENTRIC ORBITS"

What is the relationship between Jesus' mediatorial reign and the rule of the governments of this world? Do civil governments have a legitimate role in the government of the church? Many in the history of the church have answered "yes" to this question. The Eastern Church during the Byzantine Period (ca. AD 500–1500) experienced direct intervention in its affairs by the Byzantine emperors. This relationship between the civil government and the church has been termed "caesaropapism."[6] In the Western church at the time of the Reformation, "Erastianism," named for the Protestant Thomas Erastus (1524–83), urged that civil government has a legitimate role in the government of the church. This role includes responsibility for the exercise of church discipline. After debating the matter, the Westminster Assembly rejected this position and affirmed that the Scriptures entrust church discipline entirely to "the hand of Church officers, distinct from the civil magistrate" (WCF 30.1).[7]

We will say more about the proper spheres of both civil and church government in the next chapter. For now we may simply point to Scripture's teaching that these two governments are entirely distinct from one another. Four observations are in order. The first stems from two related matters: the nature of Christ's kingdom, and membership in Christ's kingdom. The Christian has entrance into the kingdom by the new birth. This new birth is not effected by such things as birthright, genealogy, or human effort (see John 1:13). One, rather, must be born of the Spirit to see or enter the kingdom (John 3:3, 5). This new birth is a sovereign work of the Holy Spirit (John 3:8). It is not in response to, in anticipation of, or in conjunction with human privilege or activity. Entrance into the kingdom is entirely a work of God: "[the Father] has delivered us from the domain of darkness and transferred us to the kingdom of his beloved Son, in whom we have redemption, the forgiveness of sins"

---

6. By "caesaropapism" is meant the state's direction of the affairs of the church. Some have objected to this characterization of Byzantine church-state relations. See Timothy Ware, *The Orthodox Church,* rev. ed. (London: Penguin, 1993), 40–41.

7. Diarmaid MacCullough, *The Reformation* (New York: Penguin, 2003), 355; Robert Letham, *The Westminster Assembly: Reading Its Theology in Historical Context* (Phillipsburg, NJ: P&R Publishing, 2009), 312.

(Col. 1:13–14). This is why Jesus tells Pilate, "My kingdom is not of this world" (John 18:36). The kingdom of God does not belong to the sphere of civil government, but to a different order entirely. Entrance into and membership in this kingdom is fundamentally different from entrance and membership in the kingdoms of this world. In light of this observation, it would be surprising to learn that the Scriptures warrant civil government's participation in the administration of the government of the church.

Second, Jesus acknowledged the independence of the church's government from civil government. One looming question in Jesus' day was how the Jewish nation was to live under Roman rule. Should the Jews accommodate themselves to Roman rule? If so, how? Should they rebel against Roman rule? Should they withdraw from civil society? These questions were pressing because God in the Old Testament had given Israel a distinct set of laws for ordering her common life. What would happen should those laws and Roman law come into conflict?

The Pharisees tried to draw Jesus into this debate. They did so, the Scriptures say, "plot[ting] how to entangle him in his talk" (Matt. 22:15). In other words, they did not ask Jesus because of a sincere desire to know the truth. They tried to entrap him into saying something that would either get him in trouble with the Roman authorities or discredit him among the Jews.

The question they posed concerns that most dreaded of responsibilities—taxes. Joined by the Herodians, they asked, "Is it lawful to pay taxes to Caesar or not?" Jesus, after holding up a Roman coin, asked them, "Whose likeness and inscription is this?" They respond, "Caesar's." To this, Jesus responded, "Therefore, render to Caesar the things that are Caesar's, and to God the things that are God's" (Matt. 22:17, 21).

Jesus is not saying that God is indifferent to civil government— "God isn't concerned about taxes at all, let Caesar take care of those!" Rather, Jesus affirms that civil government has a God-assigned sphere of responsibility. This sphere of the civil magistrate includes, among other things, the power of taxation (see also Rom. 13:1–7). Because this task is God-assigned, it is not left to our discretion to obey or disobey civil government at will. Jesus, therefore, will not step into the trap of saying that, in the name of obedience to God, we should refuse to pay our taxes.

Jesus equally affirms that there is a distinct sphere of responsibility that God has assigned to the government of his people (Matt. 22:17, 21). While Jesus does not here elaborate what that sphere entails, he nevertheless observes that there are limitations or boundaries that God has appointed to civil government with respect to the people of God. The state may not transgress those boundaries. The state's authority is therefore a limited one, and that by divine appointment. This authority is limited partly because God has established a distinct sphere and government independent of that of the state. Therefore, there are responsibilities we have to Caesar, and then there are distinct responsibilities we have to God.

Third, Jesus earlier and elsewhere appoints a government for the church, distinct from the governments of the kingdoms of this world. In Matthew 16:16, Peter confesses Jesus to be "the Christ, the Son of the living God." Jesus then says to Peter:

> Blessed are you, Simon Bar-Jonah! For flesh and blood has not revealed this to you, but my Father who is in heaven. And I tell you, you are Peter, and on this rock I will build my church, and the gates of hell shall not prevail against it. I will give you the keys of the kingdom of heaven, and whatever you bind on earth shall be bound in heaven, and whatever you loose on earth shall be loosed in heaven. (Matt. 16:17–19)

What is Jesus saying here? Before we address this question, we need to take up a prior question. To whom is Jesus speaking at this point? Some have urged that Jesus is not speaking to the disciples generally, but to Peter specifically. The Roman Catholic Church, for instance, has appealed to this text in support of the papacy, or that the pope, the supposed successor of Peter, is the head of the church. Roman Catholics see Jesus here uniquely entrusting Peter alone with tremendous ecclesiastical authority.

Protestants have vigorously disagreed with this conclusion. The Westminster Confession declares, "There is no other head of the Church but the Lord Jesus Christ. Nor can the Pope of Rome, in any sense, be head thereof" (WCF 25.6). Jesus alone is head of the church. Therefore, neither the pope nor any other individual may be regarded or termed the church's "head."

At first glance, Rome's appeal to Matthew 16 has the ring of plausibility. Jesus, after all, is addressing Peter directly here.[8] Before we conclude that *only* Peter is in view, however, two considerations merit reflection. First, Peter's confession (16:16) was occasioned by Jesus' questions, "Who do people say that the Son of Man is?" (16:13), and "But who do you say that I am?" (16:15). Jesus, in other words, is asking a question to all his disciples.[9] When Peter replies with his confession of Jesus, we should therefore understand him to be speaking for the whole body of Jesus' disciples. Second, when Jesus addresses the matter of "binding and loosing" again in Matthew 18:18, he addresses the disciples collectively.[10] This suggests that the "binding and loosing" in Matthew 16 is a matter that belongs to the disciples collectively.

What, then, is the "rock" on which Jesus will build his church? It is not Peter's confession in abstraction from Peter. Nor is it Peter in abstraction from his confession. This "rock" is the confession of Jesus as Messiah—a confession that the body of disciples has made through Peter.[11] Jesus is saying here what the apostle Paul would later write to the Ephesians, namely, that the church is "built on the foundation of the apostles and prophets, Christ Jesus himself being the cornerstone" (Eph. 2:20). The apostles bore unique witness to Jesus, God's Messiah, crucified and risen from the dead for the salvation of sinners. It is upon

8. Greek distinguishes, in a way that modern English does not, between the second person singular and the second person plural. In the Greek original of Matt. 16, the second person address is consistently in the singular and not the plural. In other words, Peter is in view in a way that the whole company of disciples is not.

9. The Greek makes this clear. Jesus not only uses the second person plural form of the verb "to say," but he adds the (grammatically unnecessary) second person personal pronoun "you."

10. The Greek of Matt. 18:18, which virtually reproduces the phrasing of Matt. 16:16, is in the plural.

11. Matthew Poole, *A Commentary on the Holy Bible,* 3 vols. (repr., Peabody, MA: Hendrickson, n.d.), 3:76.

this unique and foundational confession that Jesus will build his church through the ages.[12]

So what are the "keys" that Jesus entrusts to this foundational body of confessing witnesses? What is the "binding and loosing" to which he calls them? It is important to recognize, first, that these "keys" are something that Jesus "gives" to these disciples: "I will give you the keys of the kingdom of heaven" (Matt. 16:19).[13]

What does it mean to entrust "keys" to someone? A passage from the Old Testament helps us here. In Isaiah 22:22, we read God saying, "And I will place on [my servant Eliakim's] shoulder the key of the house of David. He shall open, and none shall shut; and he shall shut, and none shall open." Eliakim is the Lord's "servant" (22:20), and is given "authority" in "his hand" (22:21). The place in which this authority is exercised is the household (cf. 22:15).

How does this passage from Isaiah help us to understand the giving of the keys to the apostles in Matthew 16? It shows us that the apostles serve as servants or stewards in the household of God. The head of the household assigns them authority within the house. What are they called to do? They are to use the "keys of the kingdom of heaven" to "bind and loose" (16:19). The picture in Matthew 16 is one of using keys to open a storehouse in order to provide for the household.[14] It is not here a picture of admitting or excluding from the house. In view, rather, is these disciples' "administrative authority" as household servants.[15] The seventeenth-century Puritan commentator Matthew Poole explains:

> The sense is, Peter, I will betrust thee, and the rest of my apostles, with the whole administration of my gospel; you shall lay the foundation

---

12. It stands to reason, in view of the unique character of this eyewitness testimony, and the image of the once-for-all foundation that Jesus uses, that the office of apostle is not a perpetual one in the church. In other words, this office has served its God-appointed purpose in redemptive history, and God no longer gifts men for this office in the post-apostolic age. We will address this point further in chapter 4.

13. Compare here Rev. 3:17, where Jesus says of himself, "[I have] the key of David, who opens and no one will shut, who shuts and no one opens."

14. R. T. France, *The Gospel of Matthew*, NICNT (Grand Rapids: Eerdmans, 2007), 625.

15. Ibid.

of the Christian church, and administer all the affairs of it, opening the truths of the gospel to the world, and governing those who shall receive the faith of the gospel. . . . Our Savior by this promise declared his will, that his apostles should settle the affairs of the gospel church, determining what should be lawful and unlawful, and setting rules, according to which all succeeding ministers and officers in his church should act, which our Lord would confirm in heaven . . . I cannot think that the sense of binding and loosing here is excommunicating and absolving, but a doctrinal or judicial determination of things lawful and unlawful granted to the apostles.[16]

What Matthew 16:17–19 shows us, then, is that Christ has expressly entrusted authority to his apostles to order the life of the people of God under the New Testament. As we will see below, a critical part of that order is a government that uniquely belongs to the church. Importantly for our discussion, there is no provision in Matthew 16 for the civil magistrate to participate in this foundational ordering of the life of the church.

Perhaps, however, there might be room for the civil magistrate to participate in the continuing administration of the ongoing life of the church. Perhaps the civil magistrate might have a role to play in church discipline. Jesus' statements in Matthew 18:15–20 show us that there is a discipline that belongs uniquely to the church and not to civil government. Jesus envisions a situation where one Christian sins against another: "if your brother sins against you, go and tell him his fault" (18:15). Suppose, however, that the offending Christian refuses to repent, even in the presence of other Christians whom the offended Christian has brought with him (18:16). In that case, Jesus says, "tell it to the church" (18:17a). If the offender "refuses to listen to the church," he is to be put out of the church (18:17b). Such persons are under the very censure of heaven itself (18:18). Jesus is not teaching here that the disciples are "the initiator[s] of new directions for the church." Rather, they are "the faithful steward[s] of God's prior decisions."[17] Jesus is not promising the church infallibility

16. Poole, *Commentary*, 3:77.
17. France, *Matthew*, 627.

in decisions concerning church discipline. His point, rather, is that the church's decision anticipated here, when it is faithful to the Word of God, has already been made in heaven. It is only as the church is faithful to the Word that her decisions—in discipline or in any other matter—receive the sanction and support of her ascended Head.

At no point in the steps set forth in Matthew 18:15–20 does Jesus anticipate or allow the participation of the civil magistrate in the discipline of the church. Such participation would be nothing short of an unlawful intrusion. The discipline of the church is conducted within and by the church.

A fourth indication that the church has a government entirely distinct from that of the civil magistrate is found in the epistles of the New Testament, the letters drafted or imposed by the apostles of Christ for the church in every age. The New Testament shows us that the church has a government all its own. Paul, writing to the Thessalonian Christians, says, "We ask you, brothers, to respect those who labor among you and are over you in the Lord and admonish you, and to esteem them very highly in love because of their work" (1 Thess. 5:12–13). The writer to the Hebrews gives similar instruction: "Obey your leaders and submit to them, for they are keeping watch over your souls, as those who will have to give an account. Let them do this with joy and not with groaning, for that would be of no advantage to you" (Heb. 13:17).

These leaders are over their fellow believers "in the Lord." They have a specific set of spiritual tasks that Christ has given them, and for which they will have to give an account. Believers owe these leaders respect and obedience in the Lord. We have, in other words, an independent government appointed over and suited for the church as the people of God. Church and State, to borrow words from the PCA's *Book of Church Order*, are "as planets moving in concentric orbits."[18]

Before we leave this question, it is important to stress what we are *not* saying when we say that the church's government is altogether

18. *BCO* 3–4. This phrase is indebted to the "Address to the Churches of Jesus Christ throughout the Earth," adopted in 1861 by the Presbyterian Church in the Confederate States of America.

distinct from civil government. We are not saying that church members and church officers do not have obligations to the civil magistrate. Church members and church officers are just as much subject to the laws and penalties of the state as are all other citizens. The Scriptures command, "Let every person be subject to the governing authorities" (Rom. 13:1). Paul saw nothing improper in his appearing before the tribunal of Agrippa in order to face charges raised against him by the Jews (Acts 25:10). In fact, Paul told his judge, "If then I am a wrongdoer and have committed anything for which I deserve to die, I do not seek to escape death" (25:11). Paul was willing to pay the civil penalty for any wrongdoing on his part.

This means that officers of the church need to be aware of what their personal and collective responsibilities are before the state. If they become aware of matters that could subject parties in the church to civil or criminal penalties, church officers have a Christian responsibility to learn their legal options and obligations, and to act appropriately in light of those options and obligations.

To say, further, that the church has a government independent of that of the state does not mean that it is unbiblical for a church to incorporate, that is, to seek recognition by the state as a civil entity. Often and for many reasons, incorporation can be a wise step on the part of a church, and in no way infringes the independence of the church's government.

What we have been urging is that Christ has not entrusted the ordering and administration of the life of the church to the civil magistrate. These matters have been entrusted exclusively to the church. Specifically, Christ has given the church a government to order her life together under his own glorious headship.

"KING JESUS REIGNS"

We have already seen that the risen Christ exercises a particular reign over the whole world for the sake of his people. His people, the church, are at the center or focal point of that worldwide dominion.

41

Furthermore, we have seen evidence that Jesus has appointed for the church a government altogether distinct from the governments of the world.

This raises a further question—where do we go to learn about this government? The apostles play a fundamental role in the establishment of this government, but what precisely is that role? We have seen evidence in the New Testament of a distinct government belonging to the church, but where precisely did that government originate? Is the church in every generation free to form and transform its government according to its own sense of what works best? Or has Scripture appointed for the church a government to which she is to commit herself unreservedly?

These questions boil down to a single question—is the government of the church *jure divino* (by divine right) or is it *jure humano* (by human right)? James Bannerman describes *jure humano* government as follows.

> The form of government for [the] church should be left to the discretion and judgment of its members, and should be adjusted by them to suit the circumstances of the age, or country, or civil government with which they stand connected . . . there is no scriptural model of Church government set up for the imitation of Christians at all times, nor any particular form of it universally binding . . . Christian expediency, guided by a discriminating regard to the advantage and necessities of the Church at the moment, is the only rule to determine its outward organization, and the only directory for Church government.[19]

This approach to the government of the church, Bannerman observes, found widespread expression within the Church of England during and after the time of the Reformation.[20]

Contrast Bannerman's description of *jure divino* government, historically characteristic of most Presbyterian churches.

19. James Bannerman, *The Church of Christ: A Treatise on the Nature, Powers, Ordinances, Discipline and Government of the Christian Church*, 2 vols. (London: Banner of Truth Trust, 1960), 2:202.
20. See further, ibid., 2:202–3.

The form and arrangements of ecclesiastical government have not been left to be fixed by the wisdom of man, nor reduced to the level of a question of mere Christian expediency, but have been determined by Divine authority, and are sufficiently exhibited in Scripture. . . . In respect of its government and organization, as well as in respect of its doctrine and ordinances, the Church is of God, and not of man . . . Scripture, rightly interpreted and understood, affords sufficient materials for determining what the constitution and order of the Christian society were intended by its Divine Founder to be. In express Scripture precept, in apostolic example, in the precedent of the primitive Churches while under inspired direction, and in general principles embodied in the New Testament, they believe that it is possible to find the main and essential features of a system of Church government which is of Divine authority and universal obligation. They believe that the Word of God embodies the general principles and outline of an ecclesiastical polity, fitted to be an authoritative model for all Churches, capable of adapting itself to the exigencies of all different times and countries, and, notwithstanding, exhibiting a unity of character and arrangement in harmony with the Scripture pattern. Church government, according to this view, is not a product of Christian discretion, nor a development of the Christian consciousness; it has been shaped and settled, not by the wisdom of man, but by that of the Church's Head. It does not rest upon a ground of human expediency, but of Divine Appointment.[21]

Put succinctly, by *jure divino* government we mean that "the *fundamental principles* of Apostolic church government have been retained, and are legitimately applied in the circumstances and under the conditions which are peculiar to our own age and country."[22] *Jure divino* government does not argue that the church's government in every generation will be uniform down to every detail. It says, rather, that the church's government is determined by principles drawn from Scripture. Furthermore, it is these principles and no other that are admitted in framing of the

21. Ibid., 2:203–4.
22. John MacPherson, *Presbyterianism* (Edinburgh: T&T Clark, n.d.), 9; emphasis MacPherson's.

government of the church. In this way, we speak of the church's government as having been appointed by Christ in the Word.

It is the conviction of many Presbyterian bodies that Scripture teaches *jure divino* church government. Consider this statement from the Preface to the *Book of Church Order* (PCA):

> Christ, as King, has given to His Church officers, oracles and ordinances; and especially has He ordained therein His system of doctrine, government, discipline and worship, all of which are either expressly set down in Scripture, or by good and necessary inference may be deduced therefrom; and to which things He commands that nothing be added, and that from them naught be taken away.

What indications do we have from Scripture that the church's government is by divine right and not by human right? We may point to three.

First, divine right church government is evident "from the character of God as a God of order."[23] God has founded his spiritual kingdom. Christ reigns over that kingdom. It would be surprising to discover that God had given over the government of that kingdom to the "uninspired autonomy" of the people of God.[24] In such a case, disorder might very well be the consequence. We expect, rather, that God and God alone would author and provide the government of that kingdom. Such a provision safeguards and nurtures the order that should characterize any people bearing the name of God.

Second, divine right church government is evident "from the character of Christ as Mediator."[25] Christ is Head over his church. One prerogative of Christ's kingship and headship is his sovereign and exclusive rule over his people. One purpose of church government is to safeguard that precious prerogative. If church government were left to the wisdom and expediency of the church, that prerogative might be jeopardized.

---

23. Alexander T. McGill, *Church Government: A Treatise Compiled from His Lectures in Theological Seminaries* (Philadelphia: Presbyterian Board of Publication and Sabbath-School Work, 1888), 27. What follows is McGill's argument.
24. Ibid.
25. Ibid., 28. What follows is, again, McGill's argument.

There must be, therefore, some organic law—or, at least, organizing principles—found in his word to antagonize and "overturn" the fabrications of men which obstruct the progress of his kingdom. We cannot resign the prior and mighty influence of a divine polity on the liberty of men, nor admit, without a treasonable insubordination to the Head, that his Church may become as readily the handmaid of corrupt and despotic rule as of well-regulated freedom.[26]

The crown rights of Jesus, Head of his church, are therefore upheld by divine right church government.

Third, Scripture testifies that Christ has exercised his prerogative as the only Head of the church by giving to his people a government that is uniquely theirs. In the hours before his death, in the Upper Room, Jesus promised his disciples two things. He promised to send the Holy Spirit to "teach you all things and bring to your remembrance all that I have said to you" (John 14:26). Further, Jesus told his disciples that "I still have many things to say to you, but you cannot bear them now. When the Spirit of truth comes, he will guide you into all the truth" (John 16:12–13a). The Holy Spirit would then "declare to [them] the things that are to come . . . he will take what is mine and declare it to you" (John 16:13b–14).

Here is the foundation of the New Testament canon. In John 14, Jesus promised his church an inspired record of what he had said and done during his earthly ministry. The fulfillment of this promise is found especially in the four Gospels. In John 16, Jesus also promised that he would say more things, by his apostles, to the church. The fulfillment of this promise is found especially in the Acts, the Epistles, and the Revelation.

That the apostles would bear Jesus' teaching to the church remained a concern of our Lord after his resurrection from the dead. In the Great Commission, Jesus commissions the eleven disciples to "teach [my disciples in all nations] to observe all that I have commanded you" (Matt. 28:20). Since Jesus goes on to tell his disciples that he will be present

26. Ibid., 28–29.

with them "until the end of the age" (28:20), we may conclude that the observance of all that Jesus has commanded must continue until Jesus returns in glory at the end of the age.

The apostles were conscious of this unique and high responsibility that Jesus had entrusted to them. They understood that they were laying a once-for-all "foundation" for the church, of whom Christ Jesus himself is the cornerstone (Eph. 2:20). Paul, for instance, understood that when he authored his letters, he was not speaking by his own personal authority. Rather, he wrote to the Corinthians, "If anyone thinks that he is a prophet, or spiritual, he should acknowledge that the things I am writing to you are a command of the Lord. If anyone does not recognize this, he is not recognized" (1 Cor. 14:37–38). In similar fashion, Peter could speak of the "predictions of the holy prophets and the commandment of the Lord and Savior through your apostles" (2 Peter 3:2). To persist in disobedience to apostolic teaching was to subject oneself to the discipline of the church (2 Thess. 3:14–15). The epistles to the Thessalonians and Colossians were read aloud in the public worship of God (1 Thess. 5:27; Col. 4:16). In his own day, Peter could speak of the epistles of Paul as belonging to the "Scriptures" (2 Peter 3:16).

So then, Jesus entrusted his apostles with conveying his teaching to the church. Some of this teaching was given during Jesus' earthly ministry. Much of this teaching, however, was given after the resurrection and ascension. Jesus promised that the apostles would write down all of this teaching by inspiration of the Holy Spirit. That is to say, this apostolic record of teaching would be entirely, and down to the letter, the words of Jesus himself. As containing wholly and only the words of Jesus through his apostles, this record would be altogether free from error, and true in every part and in every detail.

What characterizes the church in the New Testament is steadfast adherence to the word of Jesus given through his apostles. Immediately after Pentecost, the company of believers is described as having "devoted themselves to the apostles' teaching" (Acts 2:42). Throughout the Acts of the Apostles, we observe God gathering his people by his Word given through the apostles, and sustaining and nurturing that same people by that same Word (see Acts 14:21–22; 16:4–5; 20:17–35).

It is in this apostolic and inspired record of teaching—the New Testament—that we find Jesus' provision of a government for his church. We have already witnessed evidence of the existence of this government in the church at 1 Thessalonians 5:12–13 and Hebrews 13:17. What further indication do we have that this government was part of Jesus' instruction, through his apostles, to the church? In an important respect, the last two chapters of this book will take this question up in detail. For now, we may observe a few representative passages.

First, we read in Acts 14:23, "And when they had appointed elders for them in every church, with prayer and fasting they committed them to the Lord in whom they had believed." The setting for this passage is Paul's first missionary journey. Paul and Barnabas are traveling through what is now south-central Turkey. The purpose of their travels is to preach the gospel, to gather those who respond in faith to that gospel, and to order their life together as the church. Paul and Barnabas do not simply preach and leave town. They take care to spend time with, instruct, and encourage new believers. After preaching in the cities of Pisidian Antioch, Iconium, Lystra, and Derbe, Paul and Barnabas return to these cities (Acts 14:21). Their purpose is "to strengthen the souls of the disciples, encouraging them to continue in the faith, and saying that through many tribulations we must enter the kingdom of God" (14:22).

But this teaching is not all that they do. Luke goes on to say that Paul and Barnabas "appointed elders for them in every church." Part of the apostles' ongoing ministry to the churches that Christ had called out of the world by the preaching of the Word was the appointment of "elders." Elders in the New Testament, as we shall see, are officers whom Christ has appointed to lead the congregation. Jesus is providing, through the apostles, government to his church. Notice that this was Paul and Barnabas's pattern for "every" church they had visited. Each and every congregation of believers was to be governed by a group of elders. Church government was and is a non-negotiable to church life.

Here we see why—it is part of the pattern of Christ's teaching given through the apostles.

A second and related set of passages is found in 1 Timothy 3:1–7; 3:8–13 and Titus 1:5–9. These passages fall in letters that are often called the "Pastoral Epistles." In these letters, Paul addresses two younger associates in ministry, Timothy and Titus. He writes to them about a host of matters concerning life in the church. One matter addressed in these verses concerns the government of the church. "Elders" and "deacons" are to be a regular and ongoing part of the life of the local church. Paul lets Timothy and Titus know what qualifications must be present in a man before he is eligible to serve the congregation as "elder" or "deacon."

We will look at these passages in chapter 4. The important thing for the present is that Paul expected that "elders" and "deacons," that is to say, church officers, would be an ongoing and non-negotiable part of the life of the church. It is not simply that Paul and his apostolic colleagues made arrangements for elders and deacons to serve in the congregations that they oversaw. It is that subsequent generations of the church were to follow this same pattern. This is why Paul writes to Timothy, "and what you have heard from me in the presence of many witnesses entrust to faithful men, who will be able to teach others also" (2 Tim. 2:2). The standards that Paul lays upon Timothy and Titus, then, are not for Timothy and Titus alone. Timothy and Titus are to pass these standards to the next genera-tion of "faithful men." And then these "faithful men" are to do the same for the generation that follows them. Thus, we conclude that church government is part of the biblical pattern for the church in every generation.

A QUALIFICATION

We have been urging that Christ, as the only Head and King of his church, has prescribed a government for his church. He has given this government to his church through his apostles. We find this government in the New Testament, particularly in the Acts and the Epistles. We look for the principles, precepts, and examples set down by the apostles in the New Testament in order to discover what this revealed government is.

At this point, an important qualification is in order. The New Testament, by design, does not give us an exhaustive manual of church polity. It does not prescribe every conceivable detail relating to the government of the church. If God had given us such a book, I doubt we could build a shelf big enough to hold all the volumes!

Rather, the New Testament gives the church her government in the form of principles that need to be applied. There are many details that the New Testament purposefully does not prescribe, that Christ has not expressly legislated in his Word. Reformed writers have called these "circumstances." A "circumstance," as Thomas Peck defines it, is "a concomitant of an action, without which it can either not be done at all, or cannot be done with decency and decorum."[27] An example of a circumstance in public worship might be the temperature of the room (68 degrees or 76 degrees); the arrangement of the chairs (horizontal rows or a semi-circle); or the time of the service (10 A.M. or 11 A.M.). An example of a circumstance in church government might be quorum (the minimum number of members in a deliberative body required for doing business) for a church session; how many committees a presbytery should have; or what form of parliamentary procedure a church court should use.

These matters are not prescribed in Scripture. But the church is not usurping Jesus' exclusive legislative prerogatives. The church, rather, is tasked with "the power of arranging and ordering under the law."[28] The church receives the law of Christ concerning worship and government. By that same law, she arranges certain details and matters that are indispensable to the orderly conduct of public worship and church government.

27. Thomas E. Peck, *Notes on Ecclesiology* (Richmond, VA: Presbyterian Committee of Publication, 1892; repr., Greenville, SC: Presbyterian Press, 2005), 122.
28. Ibid.

The Westminster Confession of Faith speaks of circumstances in this way.

> There are some circumstances concerning the worship of God, and government of the church, common to human actions and societies, which are to be ordered by the light of nature, and Christian prudence, according to the general rules of the Word, which are always to be observed." (WCF 1.6)

Westminster is saying at least three things about circumstances. First, circumstances surface in at least two areas—the public worship of God, and the church's government. Second, a circumstance must be "common to human actions and societies." That is to say, it must be something shared with organizations and activities other than the church and her work. Third, a circumstance is subject to certain objective standards— "the light of nature, and Christian prudence, according to the general rules of the Word, which are always to be observed."

The biblical basis for this doctrine of circumstances is found in 1 Corinthians 14. In this chapter, Paul is giving the Corinthian church standards for public worship. In the course of this chapter, Paul twice articulates the basis for the legitimacy of what we have been terming "circumstances" in the public worship of God. At 1 Corinthians 14:26, Paul writes, "When you come together, each one has a hymn, a lesson, a revelation, a tongue, or an interpretation. Let all things be done for building up." He concludes his discussion in this way: "But all things should be done decently and in order" (1 Cor. 14:40).

Scripture, then, gives us two criteria for ordering circumstantial matters in church government and in public worship. The first is edification ("Let all things be done for building up"). The second is decency and orderliness ("But all things should be done decently and in order"). In the PCA, for instance, the General Assembly has adopted *Robert's Rules of Order, Newly Revised*, as her standard of parliamentary procedure.[29] A

---

29. "Except as otherwise specifically provided in these Rules [of Assembly Operations], *Robert's Rules of Order, Newly Revised*, shall be the standard in parliamentary procedure." *RAO* 19–1.

quorum for a Session consisting of a pastor and three ruling elders is the pastor and one ruling elder.[30] The presbytery of which I am a member (the Mississippi Valley Presbytery of the Presbyterian Church in America) has several standing committees addressing such areas as administration, world missions, and Christian education. None of these rules can be substantiated by a "proof text" from the Bible. The church, rather, has formulated them using common sense governed by the general principles of the Word. She has done so because she could not undertake the work of church government without them. She has done so guided by a desire to edify the church, and to conduct her work decently and in good order.

Much of the practical, day-to-day work of the church and many of the stipulations of contemporary Presbyterian Books of Church Order fall in the category of "circumstantial matters." Thankfully, as twenty-first century Presbyterians, we benefit from centuries of the experience of our Presbyterian forebears. We are not left to "reinvent the wheel." We inherit from previous generations a body of procedures concerning church government. These procedures have already been tried, sifted, tested, and modified in the life of the church. And yet, we do not uncritically receive this bequeathal. We are free to modify it according to the Word of God and according to what edification, decency, and orderliness require. Nevertheless, the essential similarities between historical Presbyterian books of church order and current ones abundantly testify to the Lord's provision for his people, from generation to generation, in this area.

AN OBJECTION

Some might raise an objection to what we have been arguing. We have said that to find the government that Christ has given his church, we should turn to the Scripture and look for the principles, precepts, and examples set down by the apostles. One might agree that apostolic precepts are binding on the church, but question whether apostolic practice is also binding on the church: "Just because the apostles did

30. *BCO* 12–1.

something and that action is recorded in the New Testament, are we to conclude that that example is normative for us? How do we know that a particular practice was not unique to local circumstances or to the first-century church? Should we not simply stick to the precepts or commands that the apostles have given the church in the New Testament?"

If this objection held, we would certainly have much less guidance from the New Testament in the area of church government. Many matters that Presbyterians have historically drawn from the book of Acts would be off-limits to such discussions—the (probable) constitution of the diaconate in Acts 6; the appointment of elders in every church in Acts 14; and the functioning of the church-wide assembly in Acts 15, to take a few examples. If we were to restrict ourselves only to the apostolic precepts concerning the government of the church, we would have a small foundation on which to build.

These reflections illustrate the practical consequences of the objection. They do not, however, respond to the objection itself. On what biblical basis do we turn to both apostolic precept *and* example to discover what Christ has imposed upon his church?

First, as James Bannerman has reminded us, "Scripture commands, Scripture examples, and Scripture principles, all rest as regards their authority on precisely the same basis. . . . All Scripture commands are not binding on us now, any more than all Scripture examples are binding. It is not the legislative form or the want of it; it is not the use of the Imperative mood in the one case and of the Indicative in the other that makes the difference."[31] In other words, we must neither conclude that all biblical commands demand Christian obedience, nor that biblical examples never obligate the believer. God reveals our Christian duty both through certain precepts and through certain examples.

Second, how can we tell whether a particular command or example binds us now? Bannerman addresses this question.

What we learn in both cases alike is just this: Thus and thus the Spirit of God commanded certain men to act in certain circumstances. We

31. Bannerman, *The Church of Christ*, 2:405.

52

learn no more in the case of the precept than in the case of the example. The one is as binding upon us as the other, *provided we be in like circumstances*. . . . The true test of its permanent obligation . . . [is to ask] was this command—whether it reaches us in the form in which it was perhaps first given, or whether it is embodied in the obedience which followed—founded on moral grounds, common to all men at all times, in all circumstances, or on local and temporary grounds, peculiar to certain men in certain circumstances, at some given time?[32]

In other words, Bannerman argues, the true test of whether a command or an example is binding upon the Christian is this: am I in "like circumstances" to the original audience? If, however, a command or example "depend(s) on the peculiar circumstances of a given age or country," then we may conclude that we are under no obligation to observe it.[33]

Let us take a relatively undisputed example. When Jesus institutes the Lord's Supper, he tells his disciples, "This do in remembrance of me." The church, therefore, in obedience to Jesus, observes the Lord's Supper in every age. What precisely do we observe? We observe the breaking of the bread and the distribution of the cup. We do not insist that the Lord's Supper be observed "in the evening, and in a private house," with "unleavened bread," and by "men only."[34] We rightly understand these circumstances and details to be incidental to the observance of the sacrament. They are not part of the "this do" command of Jesus. The reason that we say this is because "these peculiar observances [do not] rest on moral grounds common to all times, and therefore they are not universally binding."[35]

The same process of reasoning applies to church government. When we see the apostles establishing and practicing the government of the church in the New Testament, we must ask whether we are in "like circumstances" to the first century church. If we conclude that we are,

32. Ibid., 2:406.
33. Ibid., 2:408.
34. Ibid., 2:407.
35. Ibid.

we therefore understand these examples to be part of the government that Christ has revealed to his church in Scripture.[36]

CONCLUSION

We have seen that Jesus, the only Head and King of his church, has imposed upon his church a government unique to her. This government he has given by his apostles in the Scriptures. This government will be found in the principles, precepts, and examples set forth in the New Testament. While the church has been called to arrange or order certain matters "under the law," she remains a people firmly "under the law" that Christ alone has appointed for her.

We are almost prepared to consider the particulars of the structure of this government—its officers, its assemblies, and their mutual interaction. Before we take up that point, however, one important question remains. What is the power that Christ has committed to his church?

---

36. For a more extensive discussion of this same point, see the helpful treatment of William Cunningham, *Historical Theology: A Review of the Principal Doctrinal Discussions in the Christian Church Since the Apostolic Age,* 3rd ed., 2 vols. (Edinburgh: T&T Clark, 1870; repr., Edinburgh: Banner of Truth, 1960), 1:64–73.

3

THE POWER OF THE CHURCH

E very legitimate government possesses and exercises power. Bad government exercises power with little to no restraint. Think of totalitarian regimes and dictatorships where civil liberties, religious freedom, and rights to private property are subject to the whim and will of the leader or party in charge. In the United States, however, the power of the federal government is limited and prescribed by the United States Constitution.[1] The federal government has enumerated powers. The government may not lawfully exceed those powers. Nor may it claim for itself powers not expressly granted by the Constitution. The limited government of the United States is one reason why people living under totalitarian government have risked their property and their very lives to find refuge in America. Sadly, limited government is rare in world history. Many civil governments over the ages have wielded power in ways that have been destructive of the good of the governed. The question is not whether government has power—to function properly, it must. The question is how that government exercises power, and from what source the government derives its power.

1. A helpful and recent statement of the principles that informed the founding of the United States government is Matthew Spalding, *We Still Hold These Truths: Rediscovering Our Principles, Reclaiming Our Future* (Wilmington, DE: ISI Books, 2009), esp. 81–116.

We saw in the last chapter that the church has a government. She has a government independent of the civil governments of this world. Her ascended and glorious King, Jesus Christ, has given her that government. He has done so by the principles, precepts, and examples of the apostles set forth in the New Testament.

As a government, the church possesses power and exercises power. Jesus taught his disciples, however, that this power was of a different character than that of the world's governments.

> The kings of the Gentiles exercise lordship over them, and those in authority over them are called benefactors. But not so with you. Rather, let the greatest among you become as the youngest, and the leader as one who serves. For who is greater, one who reclines at table or one who serves? Is it not the one who reclines at table? But I am among you as the one who serves. (Luke 22:25–27)

In these words, Jesus explicitly contrasts the way that the governments of the world so often relate to the governed with the way that his disciples are to relate with one another. Jesus is not "condemn[ing] the exercise of any legitimate authority which He has set up in the Church." Rather, he is condemning "the eager desire of Christian ministers after worldly greatness and glory," as well as "the exercise even of lawful authority in a haughty and offensive spirit."[2] In this way, the church is to be different from the world around her.

To be sure, the church has power. Jesus reminds us, however, that the church's power and its exercise can differ in many ways from the power wielded by the governments of the world. In this chapter we will take up this matter. We will follow the outline of the discussion of this subject in Stuart Robinson's *The Church of God as an Essential Element of the Gospel*. In that work, Robinson addresses four features of the power of the church. These four features are, first, the source of church power; second, the delegation and vesting

---

2. Thomas Witherow, *The Form of the Christian Temple: Being a Treatise on the Constitution of the New Testament Church* (Edinburgh: T&T Clark, 1889), 291.

of church power; third, the mode of exercise of church power; and fourth, the limits of church power.

THE SOURCE OF CHURCH POWER

What is the source of the church's power? In the Declaration of Independence, the American Founders declared that "Governments . . . instituted among Men, derive their just powers from the consent of the governed." In other words, the power exercised by the government derives ultimately from a compact or agreement of the "sovereign people."[3] From where does power in the church ultimately derive? Does it derive from a sovereign church membership?

The answer of Scripture is decidedly negative. Church power does not derive from the members of the church. It derives from Jesus alone. This is what we expect to be the case. Scripture, we have seen, says that Jesus relates to the church as head to body, and as king to subject (Eph. 5:23; Col. 1:18). In each case, power runs one way: from Jesus to his church.

Specifically, "the source of all Church power is primarily Jesus Christ, the Mediator."[4] We have seen that Jesus introduces the Great Commission with the declaration, "All authority in heaven and on earth has been given to me." Centuries before, Isaiah had prophesied that "the government shall be upon his [i.e., Jesus'] shoulder" (Isa. 9:6). This is why, Robinson explains, the apostles "teach in the name of Jesus" (Acts 4:17–18); administer discipline in the name of Jesus (Matt. 18:20; 1 Cor. 5:4); and why Jesus "contain[s] in himself, by way of eminency, all the offices of the church."[5] In short, the church's doctrine, discipline, and offices derive from Jesus and not from any human authority.

There is an important lesson here. The teaching of the church, or acts of discipline carried out by the church do not carry their weight simply because they are acts of the church. They carry their weight only

3. See Spalding, *We Still Hold These Truths*, 48.
4. Stuart Robinson, *The Church of God as an Essential Element of the Gospel* (Philadelphia: Joseph M. Wilson, 1858; repr., Willow Grove, PA), 61.
5. Ibid., 61–62.

as they carry the sanction and smile of Jesus (see Matt. 18:19–20). But how can we know whether any teaching or action of the church has the blessing of Jesus? The answer is: by finding out whether that teaching or action conforms to or departs from the teaching of the Word of God. When the church acts in conformity with what Christ has called her to do in the written Word, then that action must be received as the mind of Christ.

In church history, the church often claimed Jesus' authority for teachings and actions that had no foundation in the Word of God. Today, however, evangelicals are likely inclined to give too little weight to the legitimate teaching and actions of the church. We find it difficult to see past the church to Christ who has authorized the church to teach and to act in his name. Perhaps this state of affairs is partly owing to an awareness of past and present misuses of that authority. Scripture's balance is welcome. In good Berean spirit, we measure every teaching and action of the church against the Scriptures (see Acts 17:10–15). When we find that the church has taught and acted in conformity with Scripture, then we ought gratefully to receive that teaching and action as from Christ himself. Whether we refuse or accept such matters, we are ultimately and directly accountable to Christ for our refusal or acceptance.

THE DELEGATION AND VESTING OF CHURCH POWER

Christ is the source of the church's power. He delegates or "vests" this power, however, to his church. In this sense, we may speak of "authority" or "power" belonging to the church.

This observation, in turn, raises a question—one that has been with the church for much of her history, and into the present day. Where precisely in the church does her power lie? Where is it located? Who is authorized to exercise it? *The Book of Church Order* of the PCA answers these very questions.

> The power which Christ has committed to His Church vests in the whole body, the rulers and those ruled, constituting it a spiritual

commonwealth. This power, as exercised by the people, extends to the choice of those officers whom He has appointed in His church.[6]

Two points are being stressed here. First, "power is vested in the Church as an organic body, composed of both rulers and ruled."[7] To understand this point, it is important to see the church as Scripture describes her—an organic, living body (1 Cor. 12:31, Eph. 4:1–16). As in the human body, power is vested in the whole body itself. "Power" resides in the whole body, not within a particular limb or organ of the body to the exclusion of the rest of the body.

This means that the church is thus constituted a "spiritual commonwealth." How do we reconcile such an understanding of the church with the biblical teaching that the church is subject to the rule and reign of her King? The resolution to this question is found in an important distinction.

> When the Church is viewed in its relationship to Christ, it is considered a kingdom (see [BCO] 1–2), but when viewed as to the inter-relations of its members, it is "neither a monarchy or oligarchy, nor a democracy, but a commonwealth."[8]

In other words, the church is a kingdom in relation to Christ, a commonwealth in relation to herself.[9] This distinction safeguards Jesus as the sole source of the church's power, and upholds Scripture's teaching that power has been vested in the body as a whole.

Second, the *Book of Church Order* stresses that power vests in the body as whole and that the people exercise that power in one way—in "the

6. *BCO* 3–1.
7. Robinson, *The Church of God*, 62.
8. Morton Smith, *Commentary on the Book of Church Order of the Presbyterian Church in America,* 6th ed. (Taylors, SC: Presbyterian Press, 2007), 35, citing F. P. Ramsay, *An Exposition of the Form of Government and the Rules of Discipline of the Presbyterian Church in the United States* (Richmond, VA: The Presbyterian Committee of Publication, 1898), 25.
9. Of course, when we say that the church is a "commonwealth," we are not saying that this commonwealth has authored its own constitution. Rather, this commonwealth has "its constitution made for it by Christ"; see Thomas E. Peck, *Notes on Ecclesiology* (Richmond, VA: Presbyterian Committee of Publication, 1892; repr., Greenville, SC: Presbyterian Press, 2005), 86, esp. note 1.

choice of those officers whom [Christ] has appointed in His church." In all other ways, power is exercised by these officers so chosen.

As Peck has stated the matter, "the power resides in the body as to its *being*; in the officers as to its *exercise*."[10] He illustrates this distinction by considering the human body.

> The body sees, but sees by the eye. The life of the body is in every part and organ, and the life of the body controls the life in every part. The eye sees by the life of the body, and sees under the control of the life of the body, and for the good of the body. The eye . . . is *in* not *over* the body for that purpose.[11]

> The power [of the church] resides in her; it is exercised by [offi-cers]. Ministers are her mouth as elders are her hands. Both equally represent her, and both are nothing, except as they represent her. All lawful acts of all lawful officers are acts of the church, and they who hear the preacher or the presbytery, hear the church. The case is analogous to the motions of the human body. Vital power is not in the hands or the feet, it is in the whole body. But the exercise of that power in walking, or in writing, is confined to particular organs. The power is one, but its functions are manifold, and it has an organ appropriate to every function. This makes it an organic whole. So the church has functions; these functions require appro-priate organs; these organs are created by Christ, and the church becomes an organic whole.[12]

This understanding of the church means, first of all, that the officers of the church are drawn from among, remain part of, and serve the body as a whole. Church officers are not a cadre or caste separate from the

10. Peck, *Notes on Ecclesiology*, 85. The Latin terminology corresponding to this distinction is *in primo actu* or *quoad esse* (corresponding to power residing in the body as to being), and *in actu secundo* or *quoad operari* (corresponding to power in exercise).

11. Ibid.

12. Ibid., 170. Peck references at this point the argument of James H. Thornwell, "Church Boards and Presbyterianism," in *Collected Writings of James Henley Thornwell*, 4 vols., ed. John B. Adger and John L. Girardeau (1871–73; repr., Edinburgh: Banner of Truth Trust, 974), 4:272–73.

body of Christ. For this reason, it is unwise to speak of "clergy" (church officers) and "laity" (non-officers in the church).[13] This terminology has been used in the history of the church to express a very different distinction between officers and non-officers than Scripture teaches.

While the people exercise power in only one way, namely, in their choice of officers, Presbyterian church government has long stressed this privilege as an inviolable right of the church. The church, Presbyterians have urged, may never be compelled to receive an officer whom they have not chosen to serve them.[14] This right is evident in the biblical account of the church of Jerusalem in Acts. The apostles direct the church to "pick out from among you seven men of good repute, full of the Spirit and of wisdom, whom we will appoint to his duty" (Acts 6:3, cf. Acts 6:5). Thus, when we read that [Paul and Barnabas] "appointed elders for them in every church" (Acts 14:23), and of Paul commanding Titus to "appoint elders in every town as I directed you" (Titus 1:5), Scripture is not saying that the people did not choose their officers. Assumed in these passages, rather, is the principle of Acts 6:3—the officers of the church must be chosen by the people before they assume the responsibilities and duties of office.[15]

Whom do the people choose? Strictly speaking, they are recognizing men whom Christ has first gifted to serve as church officers. They extend their call to office only to those men whom they are persuaded that Christ has called and gifted for office. The election of officers by the people, then, is Christ's appointed means to place officers in his church. As Robinson observes, "In this spiritual kingdom of Christ, through the appointment to office, the qualifications and commission, are from him, the true invisible Head of the kingdom, yet the vocation to the actual

13. The Roman Catholic church, for instance, does not vest church power in the people as a whole. Rather, it vests church power exclusively in the clergy. This understanding of church power lays an unwholesome and unbiblical divide between church officers and non-officers in the church. See Peck, *Notes on Ecclesiology*, 173.

14. See the Sixth Preliminary Principle (found in the Preface) of the PCA's *BCO*.

15. See further the comments of J. A. Alexander, *A Commentary on the Acts of the Apostles*, 2 vols. (New York: Charles Scribner, 1857; repr., Edinburgh: Banner of Truth, 1963), 2:65–66; Thomas E. Peck, *Writings of Thomas E. Peck*, 3 vols., selected and arranged by T. C. Johnson (Edinburgh: Banner of Truth Trust, 1999), 3:154.

exercise of the office so conferred is in the people."[16] Peck urges the same point. "It is Christ who creates the office and defines its functions and prescribes the qualifications for it. And yet, according to the will of the same Lord and Head, the call to be an officer is not complete without the action of the church. Hence, vocation is both inward and outward; and the outward consists of election and ordination."[17]

This point has great practical importance. The officers of the church are chosen by the people. They are, however, first gifted by Christ for church office. Election acknowledges what is already the case—these particular men have been gifted by Christ for office. Election "completes" the call of Christ to a particular man to office. This means that the officers of the church, while elected by the people, are not ultimately account-able to the people. They are accountable to Christ. The authority that they exercise derives from Christ. It does not derive from the people. The officers do not owe their loyalty to the will of the people. They are not a committee of the congregation, bound to do its will.[18] Church officers, rather, owe their loyalty to the will of Christ, represented in Scripture. When the will of the people conflicts with the clear teaching of Scripture, church officers are duty bound to heed the teaching of Scripture, whatever the cost. However unpopular or uncomfortable a right decision may be in the eyes of some, the church officer may rest in the assurance that he has done what is right in the eyes of Jesus. Even if at that moment the approval of Jesus is all that he has, the approval of Jesus is all that he needs to be a faithful officer in the church.

Furthermore, the "people have no share in the government, but only the right of choosing their governors."[19] Apart from the election of officers, the exercise of power in the church belongs to the officers

16. Robinson, *The Church of God*, 63.

17. Peck, *Notes on Ecclesiology*, 89–90. Peck continues by saying, "Election is the act of the body; ordination the act of the rulers already existing, who have themselves been chosen in like manner; but both election and ordination are acts of the church. . . . Ordination imparts no authority, it only recognizes and authenticates it," 90.

18. Congregational church government can sometimes work this way. To put it in terms of our discussion, power is thought not only to reside in the church as a whole, but the church as a whole exercises that same power across the whole range of the activities of church government.

19. Peck, *Notes on Ecclesiology*, 177.

of the church. In this sense, it is not shared between the officers and non-officers of the church.

This does not mean, however, that the church is consigned to suffer under bad government. If an officer misuses his power in the church, Christ has appointed a system of discipline in the Scriptures. The officers, exercising this biblical system of discipline, aim at the repentance and recovery of the offending officer. If that officer persists in his misuse of power, the church, acting through her officers, may suspend him from office or even remove him from office altogether. The Scripture does not envision non-officers stepping forward and taking these matters into their own hands. This is part of what it means to live under the government that Christ has given his church.

It is important to stress that the power exercised by church officers is not vested in them "personally, but as representative men."[20] In other words, Christ does not cede his power to the church. Men exercising power in the church do not do so upon the authority of their own person or character. They do so as representatives of Jesus, who possesses all such power in his own person. Church officers are not a law unto themselves. They are men who serve under the standards that Christ has given his church in Scripture.

THE MODE OF CHURCH POWER

We have seen that Jesus Christ, the Head and King of his church, is the sole source of power in the church. We have also seen that Jesus delegates or vests this power to the church as a whole. We described that delegation in two-fold fashion. Power resides in the body as a whole. The people's exercise of that power extends only to their choice of officers to serve the body. This right, we argued, is biblical and inviolable. All remaining exercise of that power, however, is reserved exclusively to the officers of the church. The authority exercised by church officers is a representative authority. They act as representatives of Christ. On the one hand, church officers are not accountable to the people but to Christ.

20. Robinson, *The Church of God*, 62.

On the other hand, their actions have weight and authority only to the degree that they conform to the teaching of Scripture.

Now we are ready to take up a further question. In what way is church power to be exercised? We may answer this question in three ways.

POWER OF ORDER, POWER OF JURISDICTION

First, church power may sometimes be exercised by one officer individually. At other times, church power may only be exercised by church officers acting together. The PCA's *Book of Church Order* addresses this distinction.

> Ecclesiastical power, which is wholly spiritual, is twofold. The officers exercise it sometimes severally, as in preaching the Gospel, administering the Sacraments, reproving the erring, visiting the sick, and comforting the afflicted, which is the power of order; and they exercise it sometimes jointly in Church courts, after the form of judgment, which is the power of jurisdiction.[21]

Church officers may exercise church power individually. The *BCO* describes this in terms of the "power of order." The power of order is evident when church officers preach, administer baptism or the Lord's Supper, admonish sinners, and so on. We have plenty of examples in the New Testament of church officers individually ("severally") engaged in these activities. Such matters are an exercise of church power because the one engaged in them is acting in his capacity as an officer of the church. He is not a free agent. Such an officer is subject, therefore, to the oversight and, if necessary, correction of the courts of the church.[22]

21. *BCO* 3–2; cf. *BCO* 1–5.
22. Morton Smith, *Commentary on the Book of Church Order*, 37. We see an indirect example of this when the Jerusalem Council addresses those who were teaching that "unless you are circumcised according to the custom of Moses, you cannot be saved" (Acts 15:1). The Council admonishes such persons before the whole church by declaring to the church, "We have heard that some persons have gone out from us and troubled you with words, unsettling your minds, although we gave them good instructions" (Acts 15:24). This dimension of the work of

We may speak of church power in another way. The "power of jurisdiction" is lawfully exercised when officers gather in what are called "church courts" and render "judgment." We will take up this work in more detail in chapter 5. For now we may note that there are certain matters that require a plurality of officers. This is why, for instance, the Scriptures again and again show us that churches were governed by a plurality of elders (Acts 20:28; Phil. 1:1; 1 Thess. 5:12–13; Titus 1:5, 7; Heb. 13:17; 1 Peter 5:2).

What is the work that belongs to this "power of jurisdiction"? It is the rendering of judgment. Elders do not individually render the authoritative judgments that Christ calls the church to render. They do so in gatherings of elders called "courts."[23]

We have such an example of this exercise of church power in Acts 15. A corruption of the gospel was being spread in the church (see Acts 15:1). The dissemination of this false teaching so disturbed the church that a council of elders met to address and to resolve the issue. The council deliberated, considering the matter in light of the words and deeds of God. The council came to "one accord" on the matter (Acts 15:25). The council concluded its work by drafting a letter which it authorized to be distributed to the churches. This letter both repudiated the false teaching (see Acts 15:24) and gave positive counsel to the churches relating to the spread of this error (Acts 15:28–29).

This court of the church gathered to render judgment on a matter of concern to the church. The court rendered judgment on the matter in light of the words and deeds of God, then made this judgment known to the church. The effect of the judgment, Acts tells us, was that the "churches were strengthened in the faith, and they increased in numbers daily" (Acts 16:5).

---

the courts of the church helps us to understand why a candidate for the eldership must "hold firm to the trustworthy word as taught, so that he may be able to give instruction in sound doctrine and also to rebuke those who contradict it" (Titus 1:9).

23. Contrast, here, civil government where frequently a single person such as a judge is authorized to render judgment on a matter. See Robinson, *The Church of God*, 66.

MINISTERIAL AND DECLARATIVE

To understand this particular exercise of church power further, we need to turn to our remaining two answers to the question, "In what way is church power to be exercised?" The first of these remaining two answers is that the power of the church is "ministerial and declarative." Thomas Peck explains the meaning of this important phrase.

> ["Ministerial and declarative" means] the power of a minister or a servant to declare and execute the law of the Master, Christ, as revealed in his word, the statute-book of his kingdom, the Scriptures contained in the Old and New Testaments. No officer or court of the church has any legislative power. "Christ alone is Lord of the conscience and hath left it free from the doctrine and commandments of men which are in anything contrary to the word, or besides it, in matters of faith and worship" (WCF 20.2). Slavery to Christ alone is the true and only freedom of the human soul.[24]

No officer of the church and no court of the church has any right to draft and to impose legislation on the church. By definition, officers of the church are authorized only to enforce the Word of God. To do otherwise is to violate Christian liberty.

This is one reason why gatherings of elders exercising the power of jurisdiction are called "courts." They are not legislative bodies. They are, rather, bodies who are called to declare the mind of Christ in relation to the matters that are properly before them. In this respect, church courts are not unlike courts in the sphere of civil government. What Alexander Hamilton wrote in Federalist 78 of the American judiciary applies nicely to the task that Scripture has assigned to the courts of the church.

> The courts must declare the sense of the law; and if they should be disposed to exercise WILL instead of JUDGMENT, the consequence

24. Peck, *Notes on Ecclesiology*, 112. See also Preliminary Principle 7 (found in the Preface) of the *BCO*.

would equally be the substitution of their pleasure to that of the legislative body.[25]

The courts of the church, then, violate their very purpose when they step beyond the boundaries assigned to them by Scripture. As Peck notes, "The Bible is a positive charter—a definite constitution—and what is not granted is, for that reason, held to be forbidden . . . the whole function of the church, therefore, is confined to the interpretation and obedience of the *word*. All additions to the word, if not *explicitly* prohibited, are at least prohibited *implicitly* in the general command that *nothing be added*."[26]

That "all church power, whether exercised by the body in general, or by representation, is only ministerial and declarative" is a matter of tremendous practical importance.[27] The church is not authorized to speak to matters to which Christ has not authorized her in the Word of God to speak. The church, for instance, has no authority to endorse a particular candidate for public office in civil government. Rather, she declares the principles of civil government set forth in such passages as Romans 13:1–7 and 1 Peter 2:13–17. The church may not endorse a particular bill pending before a civil legislative body, for instance, a bill concerning abortion. The church, rather, must declare that abortion is a violation of the sixth commandment of God, and do so without reference to endorsing this or any other piece of legislation.

The Westminster Confession of Faith affirms this principle.

> Synods and Councils are to handle, or conclude, nothing, but that which is ecclesiastical; and are not to intermeddle with civil affairs which concern the commonwealth; unless by way of humble petition, in cases extraordinary; or by way of advice, for satisfaction of conscience, if they be thereunto required by the civil magistrate. (WCF 31.4)

25. Hamilton, "The Federalist, No. 78," in Alexander Hamilton, James Madison, and John Jay, *The Federalist Papers*, ed. B. F. Wright (New York: MetroBooks, 2002), 493.
26. Peck, *Notes on Ecclesiology*, 119. Emphasis Peck's.
27. These words come from Preliminary Principle 7 of the *BCO*.

The Confession affirms here that the courts of the church are to handle exclusively "ecclesiastical" matters. That is to say, they are called to declare the will of God as recorded in the Scriptures. Provision is made to address "civil affairs" in only two instances—"humble petition in cases extraordinary," and when the civil magistrate requires that the church provide advice on a matter. Even in these matters, the courts of the church would take care to limit itself to declaring the will of God concerning the matter in question, for example, "abortion is a violation of the law of God."[28]

The reason for these boundaries set on the courts of the church is at least two-fold. First, the church must exercise her power only within the bounds assigned to her by Christ. She is neither authorized nor promised competence to speak to matters that fall outside what God has declared in his Word. Sadly, many American churches in the twenty-first century have departed from this principle. Many church bodies routinely vote to support or oppose pieces of legislation pending before Congress, or policies of the current presidential administration. Whatever well-intentioned motivations may lie behind such actions, the Scriptures declare these actions to be unfaithfulness to Christ. It is unfaithful because the church has stepped outside the boundaries appointed for her by Christ in his Word.

A second reason for these boundaries is Christian liberty, as Peck observes. Christ has freed his people "from the doctrine and commandments of men which are in any thing, contrary to His Word, or beside it, if in matters of faith or worship" (WCF 20.2). When church courts overstep the bounds that Christ has assigned to them in his Word, they risk binding the conscience of individual believers.

Suppose, for some reason, that a court of the church passes a resolution that urges Christians to support a bill pending before the United States Congress. Let us say that this bill, if passed into law, will restrict abortion. At first glance, it seems commendable that the church has

28. A positive and constructive example of how the church may with integrity address such a matter as that envisioned in WCF 31.4 is the PCA General Assembly's "Declaration of Conscience on Homosexuals and the Military" (1993), available online at http://www.pca history.org/pca/2-399.html.

acted this way. After all, shouldn't we, as the church, collectively and actively support such efforts?

Put yourself in the position, however, of a Christian congressman. He believes that abortion is a violation of the sixth commandment and thus supports outlawing abortion. This does not necessarily mean that he supports this particular bill. Perhaps he opposes this bill because he believes that its provisions would stand in violation of the United States Constitution. Or, perhaps he opposes this bill on fiscal grounds. Or, perhaps he opposes this bill because he believes that, despite the bill's stated intentions, the bill will actually not restrict abortion.

This court of the church, by overstepping its bounds and making a pronouncement concerning a matter outside its sphere of competence, has bound the conscience of this believer. Christ has called and gifted this Christian congressman to weigh, debate, and vote upon bills that come before the legislature of which he is a member. He has not so called and gifted the elders of the church. By overstepping its biblical bounds, this court of the church has inserted itself between Christ and the conscience of this believer. This believer is not helped but hindered in his efforts to serve Christ as a legislator.

Our claim that the courts of the church are limited to declaring only the will of Christ from the Scriptures is a biblical one. Throughout the New Testament, the courts and the officers of the church steadfastly refrain from addressing the pressing political questions of the day. We never see the church drafting resolutions to the Roman Senate or to Caesar Augustus. We never see the church decrying slavery, economic inequality, imperial military actions, immigration policy, and a host of other social and political concerns. What Acts and the epistles show us is the church proclaiming and taking up in her courts Christ and him crucified, risen from the dead (see 1 Cor. 2:2 with 1:10–31; 1 Cor. 15:1–4).

The apostles make clear that each Christian is bound to keep the law of God, and so urge particular duties upon believers. These duties are to be followed in all their callings—their families, their neighborhoods, their places of work, and in the civil sphere. The apostles, moreover, teach that God holds all human beings accountable to the same standard to which Christians are held accountable: the law of God. All this is to say that the life of the individual Christian very much has a public face and a public dimension to it. We are not urging the believer's withdrawal from society or social engagement. We are saying that Christ, for the reasons we have outlined above, has limited the courts of the church to declaring the will of Christ as revealed in the Scriptures.

DOCTRINE, ORDER, AND DISCIPLINE

We have yet to address a third and critical matter in answer to our question, "In what way is church power to be exercised?" We have said that all church power is only ministerial and declarative, and that the courts of the church are tasked with declaring the Word of God. May we say more about the particulars of that task?

Here a three-fold distinction helps us to understand this responsibility. This three-fold distinction relates to what we have termed the "power of jurisdiction," or the authority that church courts, or assemblies of elders, exercise. This three-fold distinction is expressed in the PCA's *Book of Church Order* as "doctrine," "order," and "discipline."[29] With respect to the power of jurisdiction, then, church power runs in three and only three channels: doctrine, order, and discipline. Let us consider each in turn.

"Doctrine" concerns the authority of the church in teaching or promulgating doctrine. Here the *Book of Church Order* affirms that "[church courts] can make no laws binding the conscience; but may frame symbols of faith, bear testimony against error in doctrine and immorality in practice, within or without the Church, and decide cases of conscience."[30] In other words, the elders of the church, gathered in church courts, may not make a law "binding the conscience" (see WCF 20.2).

---

29. See *BCO* 11–2, "The jurisdiction of Church courts is only ministerial and declarative, and relates to the doctrines and precepts of Christ, to the order of the Church, and to the exercise of discipline." The older and classical terminology is—dogmatic, diatactical, and diacritical power, respectively.

30. *BCO* 11–2. As Peck observes, this aspect of church power applies not only to church courts but, *mutatis mutandis*, to church officers. *Notes on Ecclesiology*, 120.

As we argued above, they are only authorized to declare the will of God revealed in the Scriptures. Positively, church courts are authorized to "frame symbols of faith," that is, to draft confessions of faith, to "bear testimony against error," and to "decide cases of conscience."

The church's declaration of the will of God, then, involves at least two things. First, the church is authorized to declare what she understands the Scriptures to teach. Many Reformed and Presbyterian bodies have done so by adopting the Westminster Standards as their confession of faith. We find New Testament precedent for framing confessional statements in such passages as Philippians 2:5–11 and 1 Timothy 3:16.[31]

Second, the church is called to apply the Word of God to specific and concrete circumstances. The courts of the church are to "bear testimony against error" and "decide cases of conscience," that is, questions where a party may have some uncertainty concerning how the Word of God applies to a particular circumstance or situation. We have seen evidence of a court of the church legitimately exercising such authority in the Jerusalem Council of Acts 15.

The second aspect of the church's power of jurisdiction, "order," involves the arrangement of certain details relating to the "government, discipline, worship, and extension of the Church." Such "rules" that church courts establish must "be agreeable to the doctrines relating thereto contained in the Scriptures, the circumstantial details only of these matters being left to the Christian prudence and wisdom of Church officers and courts."[32]

We see evidence of the exercise of this aspect of church power when churches adopt a form of government, rules of discipline, a directory for worship, or a standard of parliamentary procedure such as *Robert's Rules of Order, Newly Revised*. This is not only a legitimate exercise of church authority. It is also a necessary exercise of church authority.

As we saw in chapter 2, Scripture authorizes the church to act in precisely this fashion. When Paul gives counsel to the church at

31. Whether or not these passages circulated independently as creedal statements, they nevertheless reflect an inspired summarization of core doctrines of the Christian faith. They therefore warrant the church undertaking such efforts in subsequent generations.

32. *BCO* 11–2. See also WCF 1.6.

Corinth concerning public worship, he says "let all things be done for building up" (1 Cor. 14:26), and "all things should be done decently and in order" (1 Cor. 14:40). In other words, there are a host of details concerning public worship and church government that Scripture has not prescribed. These are details that the Westminster Confession of Faith acknowledges are "common to human actions and societies." These details are left to the courts of the church to order. They are to do so "by the light of nature and Christian prudence, according to the general rules of the Word, which are always to be observed."[33]

Notice that this power of order is a joint power. Were elders individually, or severally, to exercise this power, chaos would ensue in the church. To preserve good order in the worship and government of the church, it is elders only acting in church courts who must exercise this power. Further, notice that this power is not legislative power. The church has no authority to craft and pass laws. The church does have the power to order or to arrange the life of the church under the law of Christ.[34]

The third and final aspect of church power to consider here is the power of discipline. The power of discipline is the "right" of the courts of the church "to require obedience to the laws of Christ." This power includes the admission of persons to church membership, including to the sacraments of the church; to office in the church; and the exclusion of the "disobedient and disorderly" from office or "sacramental privileges." The church is even empowered, through her courts, to "cut off the contumacious and impenitent from the congregation of believers." The church also has the "administrative authority" it needs to exercise these powers.[35]

It is this power that meets with particular resistance in the present day. Many conceive the church to be a mere voluntary society. A person enters by choice and may exit by choice, for any reason. Any effort on the part of the church to administer discipline, even to remove a

---

33. WCF 1.6.
34. See further Peck, *Notes on Ecclesiology*, 121–24.
35. *BCO* 11–2.

person from the membership of the church, can be deemed tyrannical and authoritarian.

To be sure, the church is a voluntary society in the following sense. Persons do not enter the church by outward compulsion. They enter when they publicly and voluntarily declare their faith in and obedience to Christ, part of which obedience is attachment and commitment to Christ's church.[36]

The church, however, is no *mere* voluntary society. Membership, as the advertisement goes, has its privileges, but it also has responsibilities. One of those responsibilities, as the vows of membership in the PCA put it, is "to submit [oneself] to the government and discipline of the Church, and . . . to study its purity and peace."

There are good treatments of the practice of church discipline.[37] For the present, let us simply observe that church discipline is a biblically necessary part of the calling of the church, and that Christ has entrusted to the courts of the church the discipline of all her membership.

Jesus addresses church discipline in the New Covenant community at Matthew 18:15–20. He begins with a "brother" who has "sin[ned] against you." In other words, there has been a private offense. Your responsibility, Jesus says, is to "go and tell him his fault between you and him alone. If he listens to you, you have gained your brother" (18:15). Discipline begins with the day-to-day and Christian-to-Christian admonishment and exhortation that our Lord expects will be part of the ongoing life of the church. If, under admonishment, our brother repents, then discipline has done its work—"you have gained your brother."

Supposing that he refuses to hear you, that is, to repent. What then? In that case, Jesus says, "take one or two others" so that "every charge may be established by the evidence of two or three witnesses" (18:16).

36. This is not to deny, of course, that children of at least one professing believer are, by birthright, members of the visible church.

37. See in particular Daniel E. Wray, *Biblical Church Discipline* (Edinburgh: Banner of Truth, 1978); Jonathan Edwards, "The Means and Ends of Excommunication," in *Sermons and Discourses, 1739–1742*, ed. Harry S. Stout and Nathan O. Hatch, vol. 22 of *The Works of Jonathan Edwards* (New Haven, CT: Yale University Press, 2003), 68–79.

Jesus references here Deuteronomy 19:15. This reference evokes the formal, legal process of inquiry that God had instituted in ancient Israel. Jesus is saying that something analogous to the process of inquiry of Deuteronomy 19 will continue to take place in the life of God's people.[38]

If that brother refuses to listen even to these witnesses, then the process of discipline is to advance to its ultimate stage: "tell it to the church" (18:17). It is now a "public church matter."[39] If he refuses to listen even to the church, then he is to be "as a Gentile and a tax collector," that is, as one who is outside the fellowship of God's people (18:17). Jesus goes on to say that when the church acts in his "name," that is, in a way that is consonant with the will of God revealed in the Scriptures, then that decision of the church is to be regarded as the decision of heaven itself (18:18–20).[40]

When Jesus says that the "church" is actively involved in the formal process of discipline, he does not mean to say that the entire congregation is called to evaluate and render judgment on this individual.[41] We know this because of the work which he particularly assigns to the office of elder. In 1 Thessalonians 5:13, we learn that elders are not only "over you in the Lord" but that they also "admonish you." In other words, they have a particular responsibility, as elders, to admonish the flock. As Hebrews 13:17 tells us, the elders are called to "keep watch" over the "souls" of the church. They will have to "give an account" to Christ for their labors in this area. Furthermore, the New Testament calls elders "shepherds" (1 Peter 5:2)

---

38. John Nolland, *The Gospel of Matthew: A Commentary on the Greek Text*, NIGTC (Grand Rapids: Eerdmans, 2005), 747. For further discussion of the judicial laws of the Old Testament, see Vern S. Poythress, *The Shadow of Christ in the Law of Moses* (Phillipsburg, NJ: P&R Publishing, 1995).

39. Ibid.

40. As Nolland notes, "gathered in my name" (18:20) "corresponds in part to 'agree together' in 18:19." Thus, a "comprehensive commitment to Jesus and what he has brought, done, and stands for is intended. But the solidarity of being gathered together in this is also important." Ibid., 750.

41. So WCF 30.2: "To these officers [cf. WCF 30.1] the keys of the kingdom of heaven are committed; by virtue whereof, they have power, respectively, to retain, and remit sins; to shut that kingdom against the impenitent, both by the Word, and censures; and to open it unto penitent sinners, by the ministry of the Gospel; and by absolution from censures, as occasion shall require."

and "overseers" (Acts 2:28; Titus 1:7). These titles tell us that this office is entrusted with the spiritual oversight of the church. Just as in Israel of old, where only a few were called to the work of discipline (see Deut. 19:15–20), so in the new Israel, elders are called to take up the work of discipline. When they do so, the "church" is properly undertaking the work of discipline.

The work of discipline is what we have termed an exercise of the "joint" power that belongs to the eldership. In other words, elders cannot individually administer discipline. It is a work that belongs to the elders assembled in the courts of the church. This point is certainly in view in Matthew 18:15–20. Jesus does not envision a single man investigating, passing sentence, and enforcing that judgment. As he indicates in verse 19 ("if two of you agree on earth") and verse 20 ("where two or three"), discipline is not properly conducted by a single individual, but by a group of persons.

This observation helps us to understand why the New Testament so often refers to a plurality of elders, that is, elders together taking up their calling to shepherd and oversee the flock together in the courts of the church (see Acts 20:28; 1 Thess. 5:13; Titus 1:5, 7; Heb. 13:17; 1 Peter 5:1–2). The apostolic pattern is that elders together take up and carry through the work of discipline in the church. The Bible never intended for this mantle to fall on the shoulders of a single man.[42]

In summary, this three-fold understanding of the scope of the power of jurisdiction (doctrine, order, and discipline) is inextricably tied to the nature of church power as ministerial and declarative. The officers of the church are authorized or empowered to declare and to enforce the Word of God. To overstep the boundaries of the Scriptures is to betray the office of elder. When the church drafts and adopts confessions, bears testimony against error, or resolves cases of conscience, she is fulfilling her calling to make known the whole counsel of God. When the church orders circumstantial matters in

---

42. "Not a case can be found in all the Scriptures in which an ordinary office-bearer ever exercised jurisdiction alone, but always as one constituting a member of a tribunal." Robinson, *The Church of God*, 65.

church government and public worship, she is fulfilling a biblically-mandated and biblically-guided responsibility. When the church takes up the difficult but necessary work of disciplining her membership, she is acting in accordance with the Word of God by addressing a church member who refuses to repent of a belief or practice that is contrary to the Word of God.

In reflecting on the exclusively spiritual character of the authority of the church, it is helpful to pause and reflect on why Jesus has ordered it so. Stuart Robinson offers a lovely meditation on this theme.

> And whilst this power is thus limited in the mode of its exercise, it also is limited as to its end, which is wholly spiritual. In full accordance with the idea of a kingdom not of this world, and of the power of men in it as wholly ministerial, is the end for which it is exercised. It is spiritual: it is to gain our brother. It is that the spirit of him against whom this power is exercised may be saved in the day of the Lord Jesus. It is for the edification of his people, and for the Lord's business; for the peace and harmony of the Church, for the extension of the Church, and for Jehovah's glory.[43]

One further way that helps us to understand the power of the church is to contrast it with the power that civil government wields.

LIMITS OF CHURCH POWER

In a previous chapter, we argued that the government of the church is distinct from civil government. We began this chapter by reflecting on Jesus' words to his disciples in Luke 22. There he informed his disciples that the power exercised by church government and civil government can differ noticeably. To close this chapter, let us reflect systematically how church power differs from civil power.

Before exploring their differences, we should note that they are not altogether different. As Robinson notes, "both are powers of divine authority, both concern the race of mankind, and both were instituted

43. Ibid.

for the glory of God as a final end." Apart from these similarities, however, "they have nothing in common."[44]

With these similarities in mind, let us observe some of the differences between civil and ecclesiastical authority, with Robinson as our guide. First, "civil power derives its authority from God as the Author of nature, whilst the power ecclesiastical comes alone from Jesus as Mediator."[45] Both civil power and ecclesiastical power, then, come from God. They come from God, however, in different respects. Civil power derives from God as Creator of humanity. Ecclesiastical power derives from Jesus as Mediator of his people. This difference in power is related to the difference in the character of both church and state.

> The state is ordained for man as man, the church for man as sinner, under a dispensation of restoration and salvation. The state is for the whole race of man, the church consists of that portion of the race which is really, or by credible profession, the mediatorial body of Christ. The state is a government of natural justice; the church, a government of grace.[46]

In view of these differences, then, we are not surprised to discover that there are differences between civil and ecclesiastical power or authority.

A second difference between power in the church and in the state concerns the rule or standard of authority in each.

> The rule for the guidance of the civil power in its exercise is the light of nature and reason, the law which the author of nature reveals through reason to man; but the rule for the guidance of ecclesiastical power in its exercise is that light which . . . Jesus Christ has revealed in his word. It is a government under statute laws already enacted by the king.[47]

God has granted, then, to the state a legitimate legislative power. The church has no legislative power. This is because Jesus is her legislator.

---

44. Ibid. Compare the nearly identical list at Peck, *Notes on Ecclesiology*, 144. Peck adds that both church and state are "ordained for *the good of* mankind" (emphasis mine).
45. Robinson, *The Church of God*, 65; cf. Peck, *Notes on Ecclesiology*, 145.
46. Peck, *Notes on Ecclesiology*, 145.
47. Robinson, *The Church of God*, 65–66.

THE POWER OF THE CHURCH

Her power, as we have seen, is ministerial and declarative. Furthermore, the church's standard is the Bible. As a creation ordinance, the state is not governed by the Bible. But the state is not without a standard that stands over it and to which it is accountable. That standard is "the law which the author of nature reveals through reason to man," or natural law.[48] This law is accessible to every man and woman by use of the mind, particularly in reflecting upon the testimony of conscience (see Rom. 2:14–15). It is this objective and unchanging standard to which all civil government must conform.

A third difference is that the "scope and aim of the civil power are limited properly to things seen and temporal; the scope and aim of ecclesiastical power are things unseen and spiritual."[49] As an essentially spiritual society, the church is to take up only the work that the Word of God has authorized her to do. As the PCA's *Book of Church Order* explains, "The sole functions of the Church, as a kingdom and government distinct from the civil commonwealth, are to proclaim, to administer, and to enforce the law of Christ revealed in the Scriptures."[50] We have reflected above on this important distinction. The church must never overstep the bounds that Christ has set for her in the Word of God.

A fourth difference is reflected in the respective symbols of state and church, sword and keys, respectively.

> [Civil] government is a government of force, a terror to evil-doers; but . . . [church] government [is] only ministerial, the functions of its officers to open and close and have a care of a house already complete as to its structure externally, and internally organized and provided.[51]

48. See here as well *BCO* 3–4. For treatments of natural law, see Michael Cromartie, ed., *A Preserving Grace: Protestants, Catholics, and Natural Law* (Washington DC: Ethics and Public Policy Center/Grand Rapids: Eerdmans, 1997); Stephen J. Grabill, *Rediscovering the Natural Law in Reformed Theological Ethics* (Grand Rapids: Eerdmans, 2006); David VanDrunen, *A Biblical Case for Natural Law,* SCSEE 1 (Grand Rapids: Acton Institute, 2006); David VanDrunen, *Natural Law and the Two Kingdoms: A Study in the Development of Reformed Social Thought* (Grand Rapids: Eerdmans, 2001).
49. Robinson, *The Church of God,* 66; cf. Peck's discussion at *Notes on Ecclesiology,* 149–50.
50. *BCO* 3–3.
51. Robinson, *The Church of God,* 66.

In Romans 13, the apostle Paul describes the civil magistrate in precisely these terms. The state, which has its authority from God (Rom. 13:1), is not "a terror to good conduct, but to bad" (Rom. 13:3). This is why, as the "servant of God" who "bears the sword," the civil ruler "carries out God's wrath on the wrongdoer" (Rom. 13:4). The authority of the state, then, is punitive. By divine appointment, the civil magistrate punishes wrongdoers. The state metes out justice to those who do wrong.

The power of the church is different. The church's power concerns only those within her bounds (see 1 Cor. 5:12–13). Furthermore, her power is not punitive. God does not call officers of the church to punish offenders, whether with or without temporal force. Some of Paul's most severe words fall in 2 Corinthians 10–13. He makes it clear, however, that he is not writing this way in order to punish the Corinthian church. He tells them that he is writing for their "restoration." He further comments that the Lord has given him "authority . . . for building up and not for tearing down" (2 Cor. 13:10).

Discipline in the church, therefore, whether considered at the level of private admonition or at the level of excommunication, is not punitive in nature. Discipline aims to glorify God, to promote the church's purity and well-being, and to keep and to restore disobedient sinners.[52] As Peck notes, the church's discipline takes on an entirely different character than the justice administered by the state. It is not "the punishment of an avenging judge, asserting the unbending majesty of the law, but the discipline of a tender mother, whose bowels yearn over the wayward child, and who inflicts no pain, except for the child's reformation and salvation."[53]

CONCLUSION

We have seen in this chapter that the church not only has a government independent of the governments of this world, but also that in fundamental ways the power exercised by church officers

52. *BCO* 27–1, 27–3.
53. Peck, *Notes on Ecclesiology*, 150.

differs from the power exercised by the civil magistrate. Both modes of power are appropriate in their own spheres. Danger is imminent when they are confused or conflated.

Remembering the identity of the church is essential to maintain this distinction in practice. The church is an essentially spiritual society. She is comprised of men and women, and their children, whom God has called out of the world to himself. These men and women have professed their allegiance to Christ as their Savior and Lord. They have, in glad submission to him, formally and willingly joined his people, the church. For the ingathering and the perfecting of the saints, they do not look to the world's means or methods. They look to the Word, in reliance upon the power of the Spirit, in order to carry out faithfully the task that Jesus has given her. The more firmly the church maintains this sense of identity, the better she will be able to carry out her mission faithfully.

Now that we have considered the government and power of the church, two more sets of questions remain. First, according to the Scripture, which are the offices of the church? What are their biblically assigned responsibilities? Second, which are the courts of the church? How are they related to one another? We will take up these questions in the following two chapters.

4

THE OFFICES OF THE CHURCH

M
ost of us have experience with elected "office." Perhaps a member of your family has run for public office. Maybe you served on the student cabinet when you were in school. Many of us go to the polls at least once a year to cast our votes for candidates who want to represent us in local, state, or national government.

It should be no surprise to learn that biblical church government has offices and officers as well. What is an "office"? How many offices are there in the church? What do church officers do? What are the qualifications for church office? How does a person get to be a church officer? Does the Scripture permit women to serve in church office? Why or why not? In this chapter, we will bring these questions to the Scriptures in search of biblical answers.

WHAT IS OFFICE?

"Office" is something that we can recognize easily, but we might have a hard time defining. This is true even in the church. Part of our difficulty stems from the fact that the New Testament lacks a "term correspond[ing] to our word 'office.' "[1] We must proceed in a different fashion.

---

1. John Murray, "Office in the Church," in *Collected Writings of John Murray,* 4 vols., (Edinburgh: Banner of Truth Trust, 1976–82), 2:357.

A foundational passage for understanding church office is Ephesians 4:7–14.

> But grace was given to each one of us according to the measure of Christ's gift. Therefore it says, "When he ascended on high he led a host of captives, and he gave gifts to men." (In saying, "He ascended," what does it mean but that he had also descended into the lower regions, the earth? He who descended is the one who also ascended far above all the heavens, that he might fill all things.) And he gave the apostles, the prophets, the evangelists, the shepherds and teachers, to equip the saints for the work of ministry, for building up the body of Christ, until we all attain to the unity of the faith and of the knowledge of the Son of God, to mature manhood, to the measure of the stature of the fullness of Christ, so that we may no longer be children, tossed to and fro by the waves and carried about by every wind of doctrine, by human cunning, by craftiness in deceitful schemes.

First, notice that Christ is the giver of gifts. Specifically, it is the ascended Christ, who is seated at the right hand of the Father and reigns over all things for the sake of the church, who gifts his church. Paul here quotes Psalm 68. In Psalm 68, David represents God as a conqueror leading captives in his train. Paul tells us that this psalm is about Jesus. Jesus is identified with Yahweh who has conquered his enemies. The fruit of Jesus' victory over sin and death is his giving of gifts to men.[2] To think biblically about the gifts, we must first consider the Giver of those gifts, Jesus.

In chapter 2, we observed that Jesus "contain[s] in himself, by way of eminency, all the offices of the Church." It is for this reason that the Scriptures call Jesus "apostle" (Heb. 3:1), "shepherd" (John 10:11), and "overseer" (1 Peter 2:25).[3] Therefore, we may never detach office and gifts for office from the Lord Jesus Christ.

Second, notice that all believers benefit from these gifts. In Ephesians 4:7, Paul says that "grace was given to each one of us according

---

2. Elsewhere, Paul tells us that "God has appointed in the church" various gifts (1 Cor. 12:28), and that "to each is given the manifestation of the Spirit for the common good" (1 Cor. 12:7). The gifting of the church is therefore the one work of the triune God.

3. Robinson, *The Church of God*, 62.

to the measure of Christ's gift." In verses 13 and 14, Paul stresses that every believer benefits from Christ's gifts to the church. What are some of these benefits? Paul mentions church unity, the knowledge of Christ, maturity, spiritual steadfastness, and protection from deceit and cunning. No believer possesses all the gifts, but every believer benefits from all the gifts.

Third, notice in verse 7 that Christ apportions certain gifts to certain believers.[4] There is no ground for jealousy in the church concerning spiritual gifts. If Christ has given me a certain gift, or has withheld a certain gift from me, then I know the following three things: (1) I do not deserve a single gift. By definition, a gift is "given." If I do not have a particular gift, I have no cause for complaint. If I have a particular gift, I have every reason to be humbled and to be thankful (see Rom. 12:3–6). (2) Christ is Head and King of his church, and not I. He is the one who decides which persons will receive which gifts. (3) Christ has assured me that I and my fellow believers will benefit from my brother's spiritual gift.

Fourth, Paul tells us here what some of these gifts are. They are "apostles, the prophets, the evangelists, the shepherds and teachers" (v. 11). In other words, these gifts are particular individuals whom Christ has gifted and called to serve the church in a particular way. Each of these gifts that Paul mentions in verse 11 has something to do with the Word of God. Christ intends these gifts to the church, then, to minister the Word of God to the whole body. The purpose of the giving of these gifts, we have seen, is to build the body in maturity and steadfastness.

To be sure, Paul addresses gifts in other places (Rom. 12:3–8; 1 Cor. 12:1–31). But not every gift entails what we are calling "church office."[5] How can we tell which gifts entail office and which do not? One way to tell is by comparing the biblical gift lists against the pattern of the exercise of these gifts in the New Testament. When we look at the New Testament, we see that certain gifts were simply to be exercised

---

4. Cf. 1 Cor. 12:11, "All these are empowered by one and the same Spirit, who apportions to each one individually as he wills."

5. Murray, "Office in the Church," 2:358.

within the church without formal ecclesiastical recognition. Other gifts, however, meant that the church was to recognize and to set apart the one possessing those gifts.[6] We will look further at this recognition below in our discussion of ordination.

There is no hint in the New Testament that a person has a higher or lower spiritual standing because he possesses or lacks certain gifts for church office. The idea that church officers are a caste of persons separate from and standing over the church, or have closer access to Christ by virtue of their office is foreign to the Scriptures. Church officers remain part of the church and are "one in Christ Jesus" with their fellow believers (Gal. 3:28).

At the same time, the New Testament does call the church to honor church officers. This responsibility is in part because the church officer possesses authority to exercise his office. Believers are to "respect those who labor among you and are over you in the Lord and admonish you, and to esteem them very highly in love because of their work" (1 Thess. 5:13). Sometimes the officer will fall below the high standards of his calling as a church officer. Even so, because of the honor of Christ who gives the gift, and because of the authority that Christ entrusts to the gifted person in connection with his office, that individual and that office should be treated respectfully.[7]

OFFICE—EXTRAORDINARY AND ORDINARY

Does the twenty-first century church have every office mentioned in the New Testament? If an office is mentioned in the New Testament, does that mean we *ought* to have that office in the church today?

6. See John MacPherson, *Presbyterianism* (Edinburgh: T&T Clark, n.d.), 23; Edmund P. Clowney, *The Church* (Downers Grove, IL: InterVarsity, 1995), 208–10.

7. An illuminating example of this contrast is found at Acts 23:1–5. When the high priest Ananias "commanded those who stood by [Paul] to strike him on the mouth," Paul says, "God is going to strike you, you whitewashed wall! Are you sitting to judge me according to the law, and yet contrary to the law you order me to be struck?" (vv. 2–3). When Paul is informed that Ananias is God's high priest, Paul acknowledges his ignorance of the fact and quotes Exod. 22:28: "You shall not speak evil of a ruler of your people" (vv. 4–5). In other words, had Paul known of Ananias's status as high priest, he would have addressed him differently, even though Ananias had acted against the law of God.

To understand the New Testament's teaching on office, it is critical to grasp the biblical distinction between *ordinary office* and *extraordinary office*. To put it another way, God intended certain biblical offices to be permanent and other biblical offices to be temporary. The permanent offices are called *ordinary*. The temporary offices are called *extraordinary*. We will look at this second type of office first.

Extraordinary Office

The New Testament identifies two offices that are extraordinary, or temporary: those of apostle and prophet. These offices long ago fulfilled the purposes for which Jesus intended them. For this reason, these offices are not continuing offices in the church of Jesus Christ.

The PCA's *Book of Church Order* puts the matter this way.

> Under the New Testament, our Lord at first collected His people out of different nations, and united them to the household of faith by the ministry of extraordinary officers who received extraordinary gifts of the Spirit and who were agents by whom God completed His revelation to His Church. Such officers and gifts related to new revelation have no successors since God completed His revelation at the conclusion of the Apostolic Age.[8]

The apostles and prophets were officers whom Christ had gifted with revelatory gifts. As we saw in chapter 2, Jesus intended for the apostles and prophets to serve as a once-for-all foundation upon which the church in successive ages was to be built (see Eph. 2:20). This foundation, we observed, is the Scriptures of the New Testament. Coupled with the Scriptures of the Old Testament, they are the basis of the church's belief and life.

This completion of the Scriptures meant that "the Apostles' work was finished and their peculiar gifts were no longer needed."[9] The same

---

8. *BCO* 7–1.

9. J. Aspinwall Hodge, *What Is Presbyterian Law as Defined by the Church Courts?* 7th ed., rev. and enl. (Philadelphia: Presbyterian Board of Publication and Sabbath-School Work, 1884), 42. See the same line of reasoning in MacPherson, *Presbyterianism*, 34. For much more

may be said of the prophets, whose gifts were also revelatory and therefore ceased when the canon of Scripture was completed.[10] The cessation of these two offices is confirmed by the absence of any provision in the New Testament for their succession. No apostle in the New Testament ever "ordain[s] successors."[11] The same may be said of prophets in the New Testament. As we shall see below, the New Testament shows us that what we will call "ordinary" officers are the ones who must continue to be ordained to service in the church.

Sometimes in the contemporary church we see leaders who carry the title "apostle" or "prophet." The testimony of Scripture, however, is that the biblical office of apostle and the biblical office of prophet have ceased. Does that mean that the church is at a disadvantage? No, Jesus has made provision in the Scriptures for what have been called the ordinary offices of the church. He gifts and calls men to these offices, and will continue to do so until his return in glory.

Ordinary Office

Which, then, are the ordinary offices of the church? MacPherson offers a helpful definition: "The ordinary offices are those, the functions of which do not presuppose any special or peculiar circumstances of church life, but are indispensable in later as in earlier ages."[12] According to the New Testament, which are these offices?

1. Two or Three Offices?

It is upon this question that Presbyterians have not been altogether agreed. Some Presbyterians have argued that Scripture acknowledges two ordinary offices: elder and deacon. This is the understanding of office reflected in the PCA's *Book of Church Order*, and has particularly

---

extended discussion of this same point, see James Bannerman, *The Church of Christ: A Treatise on the Nature, Powers, Ordinances, Discipline and Government of the Christian Church*, 2 vols. (London: Banner of Truth Trust, 1960), 2:214–44.

10. "Question: Why have [prophets] ceased? Answer: The Church has the completed Word of God," in Hodge, *What Is Presbyterian Law*, 43.

11. Ibid.

12. MacPherson, *Presbyterianism*, 34.

strong historical representation in the Southern Presbyterian Church.[13] The "two-office view" further argues that within the one office of elder there are two orders, the teaching elder and the ruling elder. Both the teaching elder and the ruling elder are elders. They are distinct with respect to certain functions, but not with respect to office.[14]

Other Presbyterians have argued that the Scriptures acknowledge three ordinary offices: minister, elder, and deacon. This understanding of office has particularly strong historical representation in the Northern Presbyterian Church, and among British evangelicals.[15] The "three-office view" agrees with the two-office view that the office of deacon is an office in its own right. It differs with the two-office view in saying that the minister (teaching elder) and the ruling elder are two separate offices, not two orders of the same office.

13. *BCO* 7–2: "The ordinary and perpetual classes of office in the Church are elders and deacons." See also *BCO* 8–5, 8–8, 8–9. In support of this view, see James Henley Thornwell, "The Ruling Elder," "The Ruling Elder a Presbyter," "Resolutions as to the Eldership," and "Presbyterianism and the Eldership," in *Collected Writings of James Henley Thornwell*, 4 vols., ed. John B. Adger and John L. Girardeau (1871–73; repr., Edinburgh: Banner of Truth Trust, 1974), 4:43–142; Robert L. Dabney, "Theories of the Eldership," in Dabney, *Discussions: Evangelical and Theological* (Richmond, VA: Presbyterian Committee of Publication, 1891; repr. Edinburgh: Banner of Truth, 1967), 2:119–57; Thomas E. Peck, *Notes on Ecclesiology* (Richmond, VA: Presbyterian Committee of Publication, 1892; repr., Greenville, SC: Presbyterian Press, 2005), 179–86.

14. For a contemporary defense of this position, see George W. Knight III, "Two Offices and Two Orders of Elders," in *Pressing toward the Mark: Essays Commemorating Fifty Years of the Orthodox Presbyterian Church,* ed. C. G. Dennison and R. C. Gamble (Philadelphia: The Committee for the Historian of the Orthodox Presbyterian Church, 1986), 22–32. See also the "Report of the Ad-Interim Committee on Number of Offices," repr. in *PCA Digest Position Papers (1973–1993), Part V,* ed. P. R. Gilchrist (Atlanta: Office of the Stated Clerk of the General Assembly of the Presbyterian Church in America, 1993), 455–97.

15. In support of this view, see Charles Hodge, *Discussions in Church Polity: From the Contributions to the "Princeton Review"* (New York: Charles Scribner's Sons, 1878), 118–33, 262–99; the Southern Presbyterian pastor Thomas Smyth, "The Name, Nature and Function of Ruling Elders," in *Complete Works of Rev. Thomas Smyth, D.D.*, ed. J. Wm. Flinn, 10 vols. (Columbia, SC: R. L. Bryan, 1908), 4:13–164; Smyth, "Theories of the Eldership (I)," in ibid., 4:167–275; Smyth, "Theories of the Eldership (II)," in ibid., 4:277–358; Smyth, "Ecclesiastical Catechism," in ibid., 4:435–519. More recently, see the essays in Mark R. Brown, ed., *Order in the Offices: Essays Defining the Roles of Church Officers* (Duncansville, PA: Classic Presbyterian Government Resources, 1993); Clowney, *The Church*, 210–12; Donald MacLeod, *Priorities for the Church: Rediscovering Leadership and Vision in the Church* (Fearn, Ross-shire: Christian Focus Publications, 2003), 41–56; Iain Murray, "The Problem of the 'Elders,'" in *A Scottish Christian Heritage* (Edinburgh: Banner of Truth, 2006), 339–66.

The literature on this question is voluminous and debate has sometimes become heated and polarized. Zeal for each position, George Knight observes, has sometimes led parties to extremes: some three-office proponents have argued that ruling elders have no teaching responsibilities whatsoever, while some two-office proponents have argued that there is no functional distinction between the teaching elder and the ruling elder.[16]

Nor are the practical implications of each position alike clear to all. Robert S. Rayburn, a three-office proponent, considers certain aspects of the polity of the PCA (whose *Book of Church Order* we observed to espouse a two-office view) to be incompatible with the two-office view.[17] Other PCA officers likely disagree with this assessment. The disagreement highlights the fact that espousal of one theory does not necessarily lead to defined practical outcomes.

Complicating matters is that each position makes plausible appeals to Scripture. Two-office proponents appeal to the fact that Scripture uses only two titles of church offices: elder and deacon. Three-office proponents appeal to the fact that Scripture describes church office in terms of three functions: teaching, ruling, and serving.[18] So great a light as Scottish Presbyterian William Cunningham, who studied with interest the nineteenth-century debates concerning this matter, confessed, "I have never been able to make up my mind fully as to the precise grounds on which the office and functions of the ruling elder ought to be maintained and defended."[19] In light of the historical differences among and difficulties expressed by Presbyterians on this question, humility and charity are particularly in order.

It is not the purpose of this work to enter into these debates in any detail. I agree with the two-office view reflected in the PCA's *Book*

16. Knight, "Two Offices and Two Orders," 23–24.

17. Robert S. Rayburn, "Ministers, Elders, and Deacons," in Brown, *Order in the Offices*, 222–23.

18. Ibid.

19. Quoted by Iain Murray, "Ruling Elders—A Sketch of a Controversy," in Brown, *Order in the Offices*, 160. Cunningham, the quote continues, held a two-office position but confessed to have been "shaken in [his] attachment to this theory" by his interaction with three-office proponent Charles Hodge (160–61). The quote originates from A. A. Hodge, *The Life of Charles Hodge* (London: T. Nelson and Sons, 1881), 425.

of Church Order. We will consider below what some of the functional differences are between the two orders of teaching and ruling elder. For now, what is the biblical basis for arguing the position that the teaching and ruling elder are two orders of the same office of elder?

The text that most clearly represents this distinction is 1 Timothy 5:17: "Let the elders who rule well be considered worthy of double honor, especially those who labor in preaching and teaching." Paul is telling Timothy that all elders are called to rule. Some elders, however, are called to "labor in preaching and teaching."[20] Paul is not saying that some elders teach and others do not. He has earlier told Timothy that all elders must be "able to teach" (3:2). What, then, is the distinction between the one group of elders and the other group of elders? If not ruling or teaching, what is it? The distinction is that "among the elders, there are those uniquely gifted by God with the calling to teach the word and as such deserve remuneration for their ministry."[21] There is a certain class of elder (the "teaching elder" or minister) who has been gifted and called to serve the church full time in the work of ruling and teaching, and who is remunerated for his ministerial labors. That these particular elders are to receive remuneration is evident from what Paul says in the following verse, "For the Scripture says, 'You shall not muzzle an ox when it treads out the grain,' and 'The laborer deserves his wages'" (5:18).

Recall the pattern we observed in chapter 3: congregations are ruled by a plurality of elders, whom they have chosen to serve them. These elders are called to shepherd or to govern the congregation. Part of the elders' pastoral responsibility, jointly and severally, is to "hold

---

20. It is worth noting a lexical difficulty in connection with 1 Timothy 5:17. The ESV renders the Greek word *malista* "especially." Some commentators have argued that the word *malista* should be translated "namely," or "that is." George Knight argues that rendering the word *malista* "that is" does not necessarily disqualify 1 Timothy 5:17 as a text supporting the two-office view: "With the translation 'that is,' those who work hard at preaching and teaching are explicitly specified as the group which should be considered worthy of double honor. . . . The designation of some among the elders as 'those who work hard at preaching and teaching' as a distinguishable group among the elders still remains the teaching of the passage on either understanding of *malista*," "Two Offices and Two Orders," 31–32n2.

21. Knight, "Two Offices and Two Orders of Elders," 28.

firm to the trustworthy word as taught, so that they may be able to give instruction in sound doctrine and also to rebuke those who contradict it" (Titus 1:9). What Paul is telling us in 1 Timothy 5:17 is that there are certain elders who rule and teach to the extent that they are paid for their service. In the words of the PCA's *Book of Church Order*, "the elders jointly have the government and spiritual oversight of the Church, including teaching. Only those elders who are specially gifted, called and trained by God to preach may serve as teaching elders."[22] For these reasons, it is preferable to consider the minister to be an order of the office of elder, rather than an office distinct from the office of elder.

2. What about "bishops"?

Some readers may be asking a question at this point: "What about bishops?" If you were raised in certain denominations, you may have had church officers called "bishops." When I was growing up in the Lutheran Church in America (LCA; later Evangelical Lutheran Church in America, ELCA), our congregation was served by a pastor. Over the pastor was a bishop. The bishop was assigned pastoral responsibility over the pastors and congregations in his region. Every year or so, the bishop would visit the church, preach, and meet with the congregation.

If you grew up in the Methodist, Episcopalian, African Methodist Episcopal, Lutheran, or Roman Catholic churches, then you are familiar with bishops. The word "episcopalian," in fact, comes from the Greek word that is often translated "bishop," or "overseer." In these "hierarchical" denominations, the minister pastors the congregation, while the bishop pastors the pastors. In some church bodies, the bishop alone has the power to ordain pastors to the ministry.

Remember our discussion from chapter 3. There we saw that the power of discipline in the church is "joint." In other words, discipline is never exercised by an elder acting by himself ("severally"). Discipline is always exercised by elders acting together ("jointly"). We are right

22. *BCO* 7–2.

to be suspicious of a claim that such pastoral responsibility resides in a single person, the bishop.

When we turn to the New Testament, we find that Scripture does not establish an office of "bishop" independently of the office of "elder." This is not because the New Testament does not speak of "bishops" or "overseers"—it does. When the New Testament speaks of "overseers," however, it is describing the elder. In other words, "overseer" is one of the biblical titles for the elder. It helps the elder to understand that part of his calling is to oversee the congregation spiritually.

Where do we see this in Scripture? Let us look at two examples. First, consider Paul's address to the elders at Ephesus in Acts 20. We read at Acts 20:17, "and [Paul] called the *elders* of the church to come to him" (emphasis mine). Addressing this same group of men, he says at Acts 20:28, "Pay careful attention to yourselves and to all the flock, in which the Holy Spirit has made you *overseers*, to care for the church of God" (emphasis mine). The Scriptures, then, describe the same group of officers using two titles—"elder" and "overseer." Thus, these terms do not denote two different offices.

In Titus 1, Paul is giving Titus counsel on matters relating to church government. He tells him at Titus 1:5 to "appoint *elders* in every town as I directed you" (emphasis mine). Paul then proceeds to give Titus a list of qualifications for that office. He says in verse 7, "for an *overseer*, as God's steward, must be above reproach" (emphasis mine). Once again, "elder" and "overseer" are terms that describe the same office.

In a recent book on the subject of church government, an Anglican theologian who upholds the authority of Scripture has written, "Earlier in the apostolic age, as is well known, the presbyter-bishop seems to have been one and the same person."[23] This writer proceeds to defend the separate office of bishop within the church on the basis of developments in the history of the church after the close of the New Testament. This line of defense calls to mind a question that we explored in chapter 2: is church government "by divine right"

---

23. Roger Beckwith, *Elders in Every City: The Origin and Role of the Ordained Ministry* (Carlisle, UK/Waynesboro, GA: Paternoster, 2003), 11.

(*jure divino*), or "by human right" (*jure humano*)? Presbyterians and Anglicans can agree that the New Testament does not teach a distinct office of "bishop." They differ in the implications that they draw from this observation. Presbyterians conclude from the *jure divino* church government of Scripture that at no point in the church's life is the office of "bishop" to be introduced into the church. They do so because of their conviction that the church's government is given by Christ in Scripture, and that the church has no warrant to add to or take away from that government.

3. Teaching Elder, Ruling Elder

We have seen that Presbyterians understand at least one office to continue in the life of the church: the eldership. They conclude that this office is perpetual because Scripture expressly lists the qualifications and duties of the elder (1 Tim. 3; Titus 1), and does so in such a way as to order the life of the church until the return of Christ.[24]

We have also argued that the two-office view best represents the New Testament's understanding of the eldership. One question remains. How are the two orders of elder (teaching elder, ruling elder) alike? How are they different?

The PCA's *Book of Church Order* helpfully summarizes the biblical responsibilities of the elder.

> As [the elder] has the oversight of the flock of Christ, he is termed *bishop* or *pastor*. As it is his duty to be grave and prudent, an example to the flock, and to govern well in the house and Kingdom of Christ, he is termed *presbyter* or *elder*. As he expounds the Word, and by sound doctrine both exhorts and convinces the gainsayer, he is termed *teacher*. These titles do not indicate different grades of office, but all describe one and the same office.[25]

24. And so Paul tells Timothy, after giving the qualifications and duties both of elders (3:1–7) and deacons (3:8–13), "I am writing these things to you so that . . . you may know how one ought to behave in the household of God, which is the church of the living God, a pillar and buttress of truth" (1 Tim. 3:14–15).

25. *BCO* 8–1.

All elders, then, are called to oversee the church, to govern the church, and to teach the church. We will not undertake an exposition of the responsibilities of elders here.[26] It is important to stress, however, that the elders are called to serve alongside the minister in ruling and shepherding the flock. The eldership is a pastoral office, and ruling elders are called to play an important role in the spiritual oversight of the congregation.

The minister is sometimes termed *primus inter pares* ("first among equals") in relation to elders with whom he serves on the session. This description is proper insofar as it describes the minister's calling to provide leadership and direction to the session in their common efforts as elders. The minister, however, does not belong to a higher rank of office than the ruling elder. He is a "fellow elder" (cf. 1 Peter 5:1).

One way that the parity of the eldership is reflected in the Presbyterian Church in America is in the requirement of its *Book of Church Order* that no court of the church (session, presbytery, or General Assembly) may meet to conduct business without the presence of a set number of ruling elder participants.[27] Often, church courts require ruling elder membership and participation in their committees and commissions. These are all ways to stress that ruling elders and teaching elders are called to serve together in a common office.

This is not to say that there is no difference between the teaching and ruling elder. These are two distinct orders within the same office. We thus expect there to be certain functional differences between the teaching elder and the ruling elder. What are they? We may note at least four differences reflected in the polity of the Presbyterian Church in

26. See Timothy Z. Witmer, *The Shepherd Leader: Achieving Effective Shepherding in Your Church* (Phillipsburg, NJ: P&R Publishing, 2010); Cornelis Van Dam, *The Elder: Today's Ministry Rooted in All of Scripture* (Phillipsburg, NJ: P&R Publishing, 2009). Other helpful treatments of the eldership include Jerram Barrs, *Shepherds and Sheep: A Biblical View of Leading and Following* (Downers Grove, IL: InterVarsity, 1983); Gerard Berghoef and Lester De Koster, *The Elders Handbook: A Practical Guide for Church Leaders* (Grand Rapids: Christian's Library, 1979); David Dickson, *The Elder and His Work*, ed. G. K. McFarland and P. G. Ryken (Phillipsburg, NJ: P&R Publishing, 2004); Samuel Miller, *The Ruling Elder* (1832; Dallas, TX: Presbyterian Heritage, 1987); John R. Sittema, *With a Shepherd's Heart: Reclaiming the Pastoral Office of Elder* (Grandville, MI: Reformed Fellowship, 1995); Alexander Strauch, *Biblical Eldership: An Urgent Call to Restore Biblical Church Leadership*, 3rd ed. (Littleton, CO: Lewis and Roth, 1995).

27. See *BCO* 12–1, 13–4, 14–5.

America. First, teaching elder candidates must possess certain educational credentials before they may be admitted to the ministry. These rigorous educational credentials are not required of ruling elders.[28] Furthermore, ruling elder candidates are examined and approved by session. Teaching elder candidates are examined and approved by presbytery.[29] Second, teaching elders hold their membership in the presbytery, while ruling elders hold their membership in the local congregation.[30] Third, ruling elder participation in presbytery and General Assembly is by delegation of a lower court, while teaching elder participation in presbytery and General Assembly is not so restricted.[31] Fourth, ruling elders are not permitted to administer the sacraments of baptism and the Lord's Supper. Only teaching elders may administer the sacraments.[32]

This last distinction in particular merits further reflection. Does this restriction not, some ask, cut the nerve of the biblical parity of the eldership? Is this not to make ruling elders subordinate to teaching elders? What is the biblical rationale for restricting the administration of the sacraments to teaching elders only?

We should first observe that this practice is one stipulated in both the polities of many Presbyterian denominations and the Westminster Standards. This fact does not, of course, settle the question. It does, however, mean that those who would urge permitting ruling elders to administer the sacraments should recognize that they are differing with a longstanding and widespread consensus concerning the teaching of Scripture at this point.[33]

Is restricting the administration of the sacraments to teaching elders inconsistent with the parity of the eldership? It is not. First, recall that the two-office view recognizes two orders within the one

28. *BCO* 21–4, 24–1.
29. Ibid.
30. *BCO* 13–1, 2; cf. *The Book of Church Order of the Orthodox Presbyterian Church* (Willow Grove, PA: The Committee on Christian Education of the Orthodox Presbyterian Church, 2005), 6.4.
31. *BCO* 13–1, 14–2. We will address the higher courts of the church in chapter 5.
32. *BCO* 56–1, 58–4. This restriction is also expressly set forth in the Westminster Standards; see WCF 27.4, WLC 176.
33. "Report of the Ad-Interim Committee on Number of Offices," 460.

office of elder. The distinction is not one of office. The distinction is one of function. There must, therefore, be some function or functions that distinguish the teaching elder from the ruling elder. Far from undermining the parity of the eldership, such a distinguishing function is necessary to maintain some difference between the teaching and the ruling elder.

Second, recall that what distinguishes the teaching from the ruling elder is that the teaching elder labors in preaching and teaching, and is supported in such by the church. Ruling elders must be able to teach, and, when called, do actually teach. They do not, however, bear the burden of the regular public ministry of the Word.

Third, Scripture not only conjoins the sacraments to the Word of God, but also conjoins the administration of the sacraments to those who minister the Word of God. Jesus, for instance, entrusted both baptism (Matt. 28) and the Lord's Supper (Matt. 26) to the apostles, whom he called to labor full time in the ministry of the Word of God. To be sure, the office of apostle has ceased in the church. We have in the church, however, non-apostolic officers whom Christ has called to labor full time in the ministry of the Word. In our place in redemptive history, then, we may analogously conclude from Matthew 28 and Matthew 26 that ministers alone are to administer the sacraments.

Fourth, Scripture provides no example of a ruling elder administering either the sacrament of baptism or the sacrament of the Lord's Supper. Each instance of the administration of the sacraments in the New Testament is by a minister. These examples confirm the principle taught elsewhere in the New Testament: Christ has limited the administration of the sacraments to teaching elders only.

While this function of the eldership belongs to the teaching elder only, it is important not to lose sight of the underlying principle we have been observing from Scripture. That principle is that the elders of the church are called, individually and jointly, to shepherd, govern, and teach the church. In the words of the PCA's *Book of Church Order*, "Elders being of one class of office, ruling elders possess the same authority and eligibility to office in the courts of the Church as teaching elders.

They should, moreover, cultivate zealously their own aptness to teach the Bible and should improve every opportunity of doing so."[34]

4. Term Eldership?

What does our survey of Scripture's teaching regarding the eldership have to say to the practice of what is commonly called "term eldership"? John Murray defines term eldership as the election and ordination of "ruling elders . . . to the office for a limited and specified period of time."[35] If after his term is expired, this individual is again elected to the office of elder, he will in some cases need to be ordained again. Alternatively, others have argued that the eldership is for life. If a man is elected and ordained to the office of elder, then this has "in view permanent tenure and exercise of the office."[36] The question does not concern whether or not an officer may be deposed for biblical reasons. The question concerns whether the ruling eldership in particular is limited or unlimited with respect to duration or time.

Term eldership has substantial historical precedent in the Reformed church.[37] The *Book of Church Order* of the Presbyterian Church in America neither stipulates nor forbids term eldership. It is fair to say that, at present, term eldership is widely practiced within the congregations of the PCA. Both historical and contemporary Reformed and Presbyterian practice, then, have made room for term eldership.

That said, there are some significant objections to term eldership. We may raise at least four. First, "when a man possesses certain endowments which qualify him for eldership, we must proceed on the assumption that they are abiding, and permanently qualify him for the discharge of the functions of the office."[38] In other words, the New Testament teaches that the church must assume that God's bestowal of the gifts for the eldership is a permanent one. Consequently, when a

---

34. *BCO* 8–9.
35. John Murray, "Arguments against Term Eldership," in *Collected Writings*, 2:351. Murray's article has recently been reprinted in "Appendix B" of Witmer, *The Shepherd Leader*, 257–64.
36. Ibid.
37. See now the historical survey by Van Dam, *The Elder*, 218–22.
38. Murray, "Arguments against Term Eldership," 2:353.

qualified man enters into the office of elder, he ought to remain in that office so long as he serves faithfully.

A related concern is that term eldership can "create in the minds of the people the notion of trial periods."[39] The problem with such a view is that the New Testament stresses the necessity of a period of testing before the congregation may elect a man to office (1 Tim. 3:10 says, "And let [the deacons] also be tested first; then let them serve as deacons if they prove themselves blameless"; 1 Tim. 5:22a warns, "Do not be hasty in the laying on of hands"). Trial or probation should precede office. Term eldership, however, may encourage an understanding of a term of service as the probation itself. If the congregation understands that, in electing a man to office, they are recognizing already-existing spiritual gifts for that office, and that this man is expected to serve them with those gifts permanently, they will see the need for trial before the election and not afterward.

Second, we have neither New Testament warrant for nor New Testament example of term eldership. No passage in the New Testament commands, anticipates, or exemplifies this practice. To be sure, we may have a New Testament example of an individual setting aside the functions of one office to assume the functions of another office.[40] Philip, whom the church at Jerusalem chose to serve as a deacon (Acts 6:1–6), is said on a later occasion to be an evangelist (Acts 21:8). That said, this example does not show that, apart from deposition, one may lay down an office altogether. The most that this example might show is that one may set aside the functions of one office in order to assume the functions of another.[41]

---

39. Ibid., 2:355.

40. This example is raised by Van Dam, *The Elder*, 224.

41. J. A. Alexander argues that this change in office was occasioned by the extraordinary circumstance of the dispersal of the church after the persecution of Stephen: "Among those dispersed was Philip, who seems never to have gone back after the re-organization of the church in which he was ordained a deacon. In the mean time he had 'purchased (or acquired) to himself a good degree' (1 Tim. 3, 13), and had long been doing 'the work of an *evangelist*' (2 Tim. 4, 5)." Alexander sees this office of evangelist as an extraordinary one, restricted to the apostolic era of the church. J. A. Alexander, *A Commentary on the Acts of the Apostles*, 2 vols. (New York: Charles Scribner, 1857; repr., Edinburgh: Banner of Truth, 1963), 2:262–63. On this reading, the example of Philip is not pertinent to the discussion of term eldership.

Third, term eldership upsets the parity of the eldership at a point where the ruling and teaching eldership is at parity: "ruling in the church of God."[42] While teaching elders may take sabbaticals from their duties, they resume their duties without having again to be elected and ordained or installed to office. No one seriously argues term eldership for teaching elders. An arrangement in which teaching elders serve for life and ruling elders serve for set terms is imbalanced and may suggest that the office of ruling elder is of secondary importance to that of teaching elder.

This point has an important practical implication for the life of the church. Term eldership deprives sessions of the continuity, experience, and wisdom that longevity of service can afford the ruling elder. Term eldership therefore inadvertently hinders the session from becoming what it otherwise could be.

Fourth, term eldership risks unbalancing the biblical relationship between church officers and the congregation. A system of rotating elders is easily politicized. Elections can become congregational referenda on the performance of a particular elder or the session as a whole. Should this happen, the session is hampered in its responsibility to serve accountably to Christ in the governance of the church. Temptations are laid before it to govern the church with a view to the congregation's political approval or disapproval of its governance. To be sure, as we saw in chapter 3, the congregation has the inalienable right of the choice of its officers. Governance itself, however, is reserved to the elders. Term eldership can unwittingly allow the congregation to step into matters that Christ has reserved only for the elders.

5. Deacon—Office of Service

The second perpetual or ordinary office in the New Testament church is the deacon. Whereas the office of elder is an office of rule or governance, the office of deacon is an office of service.[43] In fact, the Greek word from which "deacon" comes means "servant." Presbyterians

---

42. Murray, "Arguments against Term Eldership," 2:354.

43. In Baptist contexts, "deacons" frequently describe individuals who carry out the functions of an elder. We are concerned with the New Testament usage of this term.

conclude that the office of deacon is perpetual because Scripture expressly lists its qualifications and duties (1 Tim. 3), and does so in such a way as to order the life of the church until the return of Christ. Deacons are necessary, then, for the well-being of the life of the church.

What is the biblical origin of the diaconate? Few Presbyterians dispute that Scripture teaches that the diaconate is a perpetual office in the church. Presbyterians disagree, however, over whether Acts 6:1–6 records the origin of the diaconate in the church. Leading Reformed and Presbyterian writers over the centuries have argued that it does.[44] Others believe that, while the diaconate is a biblical office, Acts 6 does not record the institution of that office.[45]

It is probable that Acts 6:1–6 informs us when and under what circumstances the office of deacon was established in the church.

Now in these days when the disciples were increasing in number, a complaint by the Hellenists arose against the Hebrews because their widows were being neglected in the daily distribution. And the twelve summoned the full number of the disciples and said, "It is not right that we should give up preaching the word of God to serve tables. Therefore, brothers, pick out from among you seven men of good repute, full of the Spirit and of wisdom, whom we will appoint to this duty. But we will devote ourselves to prayer and to the ministry of the word." And what they said pleased the whole gathering, and

44. Peck, *Notes on Ecclesiology*, 207; William D. Killen, *The Framework of the Church: A Treatise on Church Government* (Edinburgh: T&T Clark, 1890), 303; Thomas Witherow, *The Form of the Christian Temple: Being a Treatise on the Constitution of the New Testament Church* (Edinburgh: T&T Clark, 1889), 82; Alexander T. McGill, *Church Government: A Treatise Compiled from His Lectures in Theological Seminaries* (Philadelphia: Presbyterian Board of Publication and Sabbath-School Work, 1888), 364 (citing also Samuel Miller in support of this view). C. N. Willborn cites John Calvin, John Owen, John Brown (Haddington), John Dick, D. Douglas Bannerman, Louis Berkhof, George W. Knight III, and Robert L. Reymond in support of this view. Willborn therefore terms this view a "consensus" view among Reformed writers. "The Deacon: A Divine Right Office with Divine Uses" *Confessional Presbyterian* 5 (2009): 185–86.

45. The nineteenth-century church historian Mosheim argued that the diaconate arose before the events recorded in Acts 6, see Killen, *The Framework of the Church*, 303; McGill, *Church Government*, 364. More recently, Clowney has suggested that the seven of Acts 6 were "assistants to the ministers of the Word, rather than officers charged specifically with the ministry of mercy." *The Church*, 213.

they chose Stephen, a man full of faith and of the Holy Spirit, and Philip, and Prochorus, and Nicanor, and Timon, and Parmenas, and Nicolaus, a proselyte of Antioch. These they set before the apostles, and they prayed and laid their hands on them. (Acts 6:1–6)

The occasion of the apostles' actions recorded here is the Hellenists', or Greek speaking Jews', complaint that their "widows were being neglected in the daily distribution" (Acts 6:1). The context of this complaint is the practice of the apostles of distributing the resources given to the church for the benefit of the needy within the church (see Acts 4:32–37, especially verse 35).

Scripture does not fault the apostles for partiality or mismanagement. The apostles, however, see that the *status quo* must change. The church has grown to the point that the apostles recognize that they can no longer both "preach . . . the word of God" and "serve tables" (Acts 6:2).

The apostles then invite the congregation to choose "seven men" who possess demonstrated spiritual qualifications. Upon election, the apostles will "appoint," that is, set apart with "pray[er]" and the la[ying on of] hands," these men to the "duty" of "serv[ing] tables," while the apostles continue in their ministry of prayer and preaching.

Several matters merit observation in this passage. First, in view in this passage is the institution of an office. The congregation chooses seven men. These men must be known to possess certain spiritual gifts. Upon election, these men are set apart to their task by prayer and the laying on of hands. Even though the title "deacon" or word "office" are not expressly used in Acts 6:1–6, the concepts underlying these words are very much present. The task to which these men are called ("serving tables") is described using a word to which the word "deacon" is very closely related.[46] The qualification, election, and setting apart of these men all point to the establishment of an office in the church.

Second, the office of deacon is a spiritual office. We see in Acts 6 and we see in 1 Timothy 3:8–12 that deacons must be spiritually gifted

---

46. The word used here is the Greek infinitive *diakonein*. The word Paul uses in 1 Tim. 3 to describe these officers is the Greek noun *diakonos*. These words are formed from the same Greek root.

to undertake the duties and responsibilities of this office. Deacons handle money and assist the poor and needy within the church. Scripture reminds us that this is a task that requires the special gifting of a man by the Holy Spirit. The church needs, to be sure, men who are practical and wise in temporal affairs. The church, however, must see to it that these men demonstrate the sort of wisdom and practicality that accompany and manifest genuine godliness.

Third, the work of the deacon is a spiritual task. The work to which the deacons are called here is not a new work. It is a work that has been going on since the day of Pentecost (see Acts 2:42–47; 4:32–37). The assistance of those in the church who were in need is an expression of the fellowship of the church. Just as believers communed with one another "in the apostles' teaching and in breaking of bread and in prayers" (Acts 2:42), so also they communed with one another in "outward things."[47] The deacons' calling is to assist the church in giving expression to the communion of saints. In Acts 6, the specific task is caring for needy widows. Diaconal ministry, then, is a work conducted for God's people. As the PCA's *Book of Church Order* puts it, "Th[is] office is one of sympathy and service, after the example of the Lord Jesus; it expresses also the communion of saints, especially in their helping one another in time of need."[48]

This point has practical importance in the church. The deacons are called to serve the church, not the world at large.[49] The diaconate is Jesus' provision for the communion of the saints. The office is designed, in part, to help relieve tangibly the needs and wants of Christians who demonstrate genuine need.

Recall that those who stood in need in Acts 6 were "widows." A few decades later, Paul wrote instructions to Timothy concerning how the church is to care for widows (1 Tim. 5:3–16). Paul, then, is giving us a

---

47. Peck, *Notes on Ecclesiology*, 207. Peck here quotes WCF 26.2: "in relieving each other in outward things according to their several abilities and necessities."

48. *BCO* 9–1.

49. See here Leonard J. Coppes's account of the debate within the Orthodox Presbyterian Church concerning the scope of those whom the diaconate is biblically called to serve: "The Discussion of the Theology of the Diaconate," in *Pressing toward the Mark*, 427–34.

window into how the deacons should conduct their ministry. Without looking at all the details of that passage, a few matters stand out. Paul, first of all, expects that needs in the church should be met by individual family members (5:4, 8). Paul considers shirking this duty a "den[ial of] the faith," and evidence that such an individual is "worse than an unbeliever" (5:8).[50] It is not the church's duty, then, to meet every temporal need represented within the congregation. The family is the primary instrument of such assistance.

Second, Paul stresses that only qualified church members may receive congregational assistance (5:3, 5, 16). Third, Paul lists several qualifications of those who are eligible to receive diaconal assistance. Implied is that the deacons will undertake a process of public and prolonged examination to establish who are and who are not qualified widows. Fourth, Paul stresses the spiritual dangers of the church maintaining church members who do not meet these criteria (5:7, 11–14). Younger widows in particular are to be counseled to pursue marriage and childbearing, their creational calling (5:14; 2:15). Paul's point is that the church must never promote, encourage, or enable ungodly behavior by her benevolences.

We are not saying that the deacons may not offer counsel and encouragement to Christians to help the poor both inside and outside the congregation, or that, in their capacity as individual Christians, deacons ought not to relieve the outward needs of their neighbor (Gal. 6:10). Nor are we saying that under no circumstances may congregational funds be employed for the temporal assistance of non-members. We are saying, however, that the proper object of diaconal ministry is the membership of the visible church. This is so because "the prime aspect . . . of the office of deacon is that of a representative of the communion of saints."[51]

What are some of the other tasks that Scripture assigns to the deacons? In addition to assisting the outward needs of persons within the congregation, deacons also serve as "fiscal agents" and "property

50. By "worse than an unbeliever," Paul means that even unbelievers recognize and carry out the responsibilities that they have toward their parents and grandparents.
51. Peck, *Notes on Ecclesiology*, 207.

managers."[52] These duties are evident by reflecting on the nature of the task that the apostles assign to the deacons in Acts 6:1–6.

> It is certain that the reason assigned by the Apostles for ordering their [i.e., the deacons'] election applies just as strongly to the collection and disbursement of funds for one purpose as for another. Their purpose was not to get rid of attending to the poor, but to get rid of secular distractions. . . . What would they have gained by divesting themselves of the care of the poor, and continuing to be perplexed with the collection of funds for all other purposes? It must be perfectly obvious to every candid mind that the entire secular business of the Church was entrusted to the Deacons.[53]

Matters concerning property and money, then, fall within the biblical scope of the duties assigned to deacons.

A fourth observation which we may draw from Acts 6 is that the task of the deacons is described as "serving tables" (6:2), whereas the task of the apostles is "prayer and the ministry of the word" (6:4). English translations sometimes obscure a connection between these two statements in the Greek text. The verb "serve" is used of the deacons (*diakonein*), and a noun drawn from the same Greek root is used of the apostles (*diakonia*). The ministry of the Word and diaconal ministry, in other words, are both legitimate forms of service within the church of Jesus Christ. In describing the deacons' work as "serving tables," the apostles in no way demean the task or minimize its importance within the church. On the contrary, they uphold it as a legitimate, noble, and important part of the church's ministry.

Fifth, the work of the diaconate is undertaken not by a single man but by a group of men who work together. Just as elders are to work together in many of their appointed tasks, so also deacons must work together in many of their appointed tasks. This is why Presbyterians arrange for the formal organization of the deacons into a Board (see *BCO* 9–4).

52. The terms are Willborn's, "The Deacon," 191, 193. See *BCO* 9–2.
53. James Henley Thornwell, "Argument against Church-Boards Answered," in *Collected Writings*, 4:201, quoted at Willborn, "The Deacon," 193.

Sixth, deacons serve the whole church. As Peck notes, "it is plain that the original deacons were not confined in their ministrations to a single congregation (Acts vi.), unless we suppose with the Independents that there was but one congregation in Jerusalem."[54] While deacons primarily serve the congregations who have elected and called them to service, they ought to be available to serve the church more broadly when called upon to do so.[55]

6. The Deacons' Relationship with the Elders

We have seen that there are two permanent offices within the church, elder and deacon. The elder is an office of rule, while the deacon is an office of service. It is a plurality of elders and deacons that serves the local congregation (Phil. 1:1). At this local level, these elders are organized into what Presbyterians have called a "session."[56] Deacons are organized into what the Presbyterian Church in America terms a "board."

This state of affairs raises the question of the relationship between the elders and the deacons within the church. Who has final say in any common matters that come before each body? Where, to borrow Harry S. Truman's phrase, does the "buck stop"? Here we enter what has been called "one of the most debated subjects in connection with the office of deacon," and can offer no more than some broad biblical principles touching this matter.[57]

It is important to recognize that the office of deacon is an office in its own right. This office is not, as it later became in church history, a "lower grade of the ministerial office."[58] The diaconate is a permanent and apostolically appointed institution in the church of Christ, and is distinct from the eldership. This office must be filled by men whom Christ has spiritually gifted for the work of that office (1 Tim. 3). The

---

54. Peck, *Notes on Ecclesiology*, 213–14.

55. See here the provisions of *BCO* 9–5 and 9–6. *Pace* Witherow, *The Form of the Christian Temple*, 89.

56. The word "session" derives from the Latin word for "to sit." Elders are those who "sit" in governance of the church.

57. The quote is from Peter Y. De Jong, *The Ministry of Mercy for Today* (Grand Rapids: Baker, 1952), referenced at Willborn, "The Deacon," 196.

58. MacPherson, *Presbyterianism*, 99. See MacPherson's discussion of this point at 98–100.

work of this office is, by design, distinct from the work of the ministry of the Word (Acts 6). Deacons must be chosen by the congregation and formally set apart to the work to which they have been "appointed" (Acts 6). Deacons are called and set apart with a view to the permanent exercise of their diaconal gifts within the church.

If Christ has established these two offices in the church, we expect that their respective spheres of responsibility will differ from one another.[59] This difference is what we witness in Scripture. The diaconate is an office of service; the eldership is an office of rule. This means that matters of governance properly belong to the session, and that the Board of Deacons is "under the supervision and authority of the Session."[60] The calling of the session to govern the church means that the elders have final say in the disbursement of any funds that belong to or have been contributed to the church.[61]

To say that the deacons are under the supervision and oversight of the session is in no way to challenge the dignity and authority that belong to their office. As McGill puts it, "The superintendence must not be dictatorial nor the service a slavery: the independence of office at the lower degree is the same as that of the higher degree."[62] Diaconal independence, as we saw from Acts 6, is critical to the proper functioning of the eldership. Deacons take up their work precisely so that the elders will not be distracted from their work of prayer and the ministry of the Word.[63] When the diaconate and eldership labor within their biblical bounds, each thereby supports and encourages the work of the other. Each office will work in its own way to the upbuilding of the body of Christ.

59. As Willborn notes, "It simply does not make good sense that what God has given to a specific office should be routinely performed by another; conflict would be certain, confusion would abound, and the work of both would suffer." "The Deacon," 197.

60. *BCO* 9–2.

61. Peck, *Notes on Ecclesiology*, 213. For biblical support, Peck notes that "the contributions of the primitive church [were] laid 'at the feet of the apostles' (Acts iv. 35, 37; v. 2)," *ibid*. See the provisions for sessional oversight of the diaconate at *BCO* 9–4.

62. McGill, *Church Government*, 368.

63. Thornwell, "Argument against Church-Boards Answered," *Collected Writings*, 4:155, cited at Willborn, "The Deacon," 197.

7. Ordination

We have been reflecting on the two permanent offices in the church, elder and deacon. Let us now directly take up the question how one enters office.[64] We have already seen that a candidate for office must possess and be known by the church to possess spiritual gifts for that office (1 Tim. 3; Titus 1). There is, in other words, a period of testing in which the congregation forms a judgment regarding a candidate's giftedness and preparedness for office (1 Tim. 3:10; 5:22).

The candidate must not only possess gifts for office, he must also be willing to serve (1 Tim. 3:1; 1 Peter 5:2). He should not enter office from a sense of social obligation or from a desire for personal gain. As one ordination vow for the office of teaching elder asks the candidate, "Have you been induced, as far as you know your own heart, to seek [this] office . . . from love to God and a sincere desire to promote His glory in the Gospel of His Son?"[65] Surely this question may be adapted for the self-examination of any candidate seeking office in the church.

Gifts and willingness are not sufficient to admit a man to the exercise of office.[66] To exercise office, a man must first be chosen by the church to serve the church as an officer in some definite work.[67] Upon election, he must be formally set apart to office by a court of the church.

64. See McGill, *Church Government*, 404.

65. *BCO* 21–6.

66. As Bannerman notes, "the title to the possession of the ministerial office is conferred by the call of Christ," but "the title to the *exercise* of the ministerial office is, in ordinary circumstances, conferred by Christ through the call of the Church." *The Church of Christ*, 1:428, 430; emphasis Bannerman's.

67. Ordinarily, he must be chosen by the congregation. Church planting, foreign missions, denominational coordinator positions, and seminary teaching are examples of ecclesiastical ministries to which, for example, a presbytery may legitimately call a man. See *BCO* 8–4, 8–6, 8–7, and the important discussions at McGill, *Church Government*, 416–17, and Bannerman, *The Church of Christ*, 1:433–35. Bannerman observes that "the title to the *pastoral* office in addition to the *ministerial* office requires to be confirmed by the consent or election of the members of the congregation over whom the minister is appointed." *The Church of Christ*, 1:433; emphasis Bannerman's.

The church must call a man to a definite work, *BCO* 17–3. The Scripture warrants and furnishes examples only of men who are ordained to a definite work. It does not permit the admission of a man to office without a particular call.

This setting apart to office is called "ordination." The PCA's *Book of Church Order* defines ordination as "the authoritative admission of one duly called to an office in the Church of God, accompanied with prayer and the laying on of hands, to which it is proper to add the giving of the right hand of fellowship." Since ordination is to office, ordination acknowledges that the person ordained has the authority and power to exercise the office to which he has been ordained.[68]

Three observations are in order. First, we see in Scripture examples of ordination to the offices of both deacon and elder. We have already considered Acts 6, where the "seven men" were "set before the apostles, and [the apostles] prayed and laid their hands on them." The seven were therefore set apart to the work to which the church had called them. They were solemnly admitted to the office of deacon. This practice is what we mean by "ordination."

In similar fashion, Barnabas and Saul, called by the church at Antioch to the ministry of the Word, are ordained. The Holy Spirit directs the church to "set apart for me Barnabas and Saul for the work to which I have called them" (13:2). The "prophets and teachers" of the church at Antioch, "after fasting and praying . . . laid their hands on [Barnabas and Saul] and sent them off" (13:1, 3).

Second, in both Acts 6 and Acts 13, the ones who ordain these men are themselves elders of the church. Paul reminds Timothy of the "council of elders [who] laid their hands on you" (1 Tim. 4:14). Ordination, then,

---

68. In *Aaron's Rod Blossoming*, George Gillespie argues that ordination "standeth in the mission of the deputation of a man to an ecclesiastical function with power and authority to perform the same" and that "the essential act of ordination [is] a simple deputation and application of a minister to his ministerial function with power to perform it." Samuel Miller expressed the same view in *The Ruling Elder*. He defined ordination as "that solemn rite, or act, by which a candidate for any office in the Church of Christ, is authoritatively designated to that office, by those who are clothed with power for that purpose" (275). Upon ordination, the elder is "fully invested with the office, and with all the powers and privileges which it includes" (291). Therefore, "ordination is an act not only official, but also *authoritative*" (292; emphasis Miller's). The preceding quotes are found at the "Report of the Committee on Women in Church Office Submitted to the Fifth-fifth General Assembly," in *Minutes of the Fifty-Fifth General Assembly . . . of the Orthodox Presbyterian Church* (Philadelphia: The Orthodox Presbyterian Church, 1988), 325, 326. Peck observes that "ordination imparts no authority, it only recognizes and authenticates it." *Notes on Ecclesiology*, 90.

is by a court of the church.[69] Ordination is neither by the congregation generally, nor by a single officer of the church.[70]

Third, ordination does not, as some in the church have taught, "confer on the party ordained an indelible 'character,' conveying to him, independently altogether of his faith in the matter or of his general spiritual condition, supernatural graces and priestly power *ex opere operato*; upon which the validity of his ministry and of his dispensation of Word and Sacrament depends."[71] Ordination is not a sacrament. The laying on of hands does not confer graces or gifts to the candidate to equip him for ministry.[72] The laying on of hands is "the gesture of recognition," a public indication that the man being ordained is called of God to this particular ministry.[73] It is "the expression of a belief that the necessary endowments of grace are present in the individual presented."[74]

At the same time, Bannerman notes, ordination is "a Divine appointment." It is not a human contrivance. When ordination is "done in a right spirit," therefore, we may expect that it "will not be without the presence and the peace of Christ, owning His own institution and blessing His own ordinance."[75]

8. Women in Office

One final question regarding the ordinary offices of the church is whether these offices are open to men only, or whether men and women

---

69. There seems to be no biblical warrant, then, for prohibiting ruling elders from laying hands on a candidate for ordination. The question of whether ruling elders may so participate in ordination was widely discussed and debated in the nineteenth century.

70. The former reflects the practice of some Congregationalists; the latter the practice of Roman Catholicism and Episcopalianism.

71. Bannerman, *The Church of Christ*, 1:472, referencing the teaching of Tridentine Roman Catholicism.

72. Paul does not say, in 1 Tim. 4:14, that ordination conferred "the gift" that Timothy has. Paul, rather, associates the "gift" with "prophecy," that is, "the prophecies previously made about you" (1:18). As George W. Knight III observes, "The testimony of the prophecy points to that inner reality," and "the prophecy was obediently accompanied by laying on of hands." *The Pastoral Epistles: A Commentary on the Greek Text*, NIGTC (Grand Rapids: Eerdmans, 1992), 208–9.

73. McGill, *Church Government*, 417–18. See the practical conclusions that McGill draws from the laying on of hands at 422–32.

74. MacPherson, *Presbyterianism*, 32.

75. Bannerman, *The Church of Christ*, 1:472.

may serve in the office of elder and deacon. It is an understatement to say that this is a sensitive issue in the church today. Since our commitment is to Scripture, it is there that we will turn for guidance and direction. Let us take up each office separately.

Elder. May women serve as elders? To put the question another way, does Scripture indicate that God gifts and calls women to the exercise of the office of elder in the church? To answer that question let us consider Paul's teaching in 1 Timothy 2:11–15.

> Let a woman learn quietly with all submissiveness. I do not permit a woman to teach or to exercise authority over a man; rather, she is to remain quiet. For Adam was formed first, then Eve; and Adam was not deceived, but the woman was deceived and became a transgressor. Yet she will be saved through childbearing—if they continue in faith and love and holiness, and self-control.

These instructions come in a section of this epistle where Paul is telling Timothy how the public worship of God ought to look in the church (1 Tim. 2:1–15). He tells Timothy that, when the church gathers for worship, men have certain obligations (2:8), and women have certain obligations (2:9–15).

What are the obligations of Christian women in public worship? Positively, Paul stresses that women are to "learn quietly with all submissiveness" (2:11). Paul upholds the identity and dignity of every Christian woman as a disciple of Christ. She is entitled to learn from Christ and called to grow in the knowledge of God.

Negatively, women are not to "teach" in the public worship of God. Paul does not forbid women from teaching altogether. Even within the church, older women are privately to teach younger women (Titus 2:3–5), and Priscilla, with her husband Aquila, gave private instruction to the teacher Apollos (Acts 18:26). The teaching that Paul has in mind in this passage, however, is the teaching that transpires when the church gathers for the public worship of God.

Some may object at this point, " But what about prophetesses? What about the examples we have in Scripture of women prophesying?" In reply, we may affirm indeed that Scripture affords multiple examples of women prophesying. At the same time, we should also note that Scripture is entirely consistent with itself in acknowledging the prophesying of women but forbidding women from teaching the Word of God in the public worship of God. Prophesying and teaching are both word gifts, but with a critical difference. Prophesying is a revelatory gift—the prophet is the instrument through which God speaks his Word to the church. Teaching is not a revelatory gift—the teacher explains and applies what God has already said in his Word. While God has allowed women to be instruments of revelation, he does not permit them to teach that revelation in the public worship of God.

Furthermore, Paul says, women are not "to exercise authority over a man." In view here is "a leadership role or function in the church."[76] In forbidding women from exercising the role or function of leadership in the church, however, Paul thereby forbids women from possessing the title or office of leadership in the church.[77]

Thus, Paul restricts women from teaching in the public worship of God and from exercising authority within the congregation. In doing so, Paul excludes women from the title or exercise of the office of elder. When we turn to 1 Timothy 3:1 and following, we see that "Paul orders and makes positive provision for the teaching and rule he has just prohibited to women."[78] Elders must be gifted to teach and are called to teach (1 Tim. 3:2). Elders must be gifted to rule and are called to rule in the church (1 Tim. 3:2, 5). It is within these positive provisions, we may furthermore note, that Paul limits the office of elder to men only (1 Tim. 3:2; Titus 1:6).

Perhaps, some say, Paul is giving instructions of limited duration or of limited geographical reach. Because of circumstances peculiar to the church in Ephesus at this time, Paul is laying down instructions in 1 Timothy 2:12–15 that do not apply to the broader church or to the church in every age. This possibility is excluded by what Paul says in

76. Knight, *The Pastoral Epistles*, 142.
77. Ibid.
78. "Report of the Committee on Women in Church Office," 330.

verses 13–14: "For Adam was formed first, then Eve; and Adam was not deceived, but the woman was deceived and became a transgressor." In speaking thus, "Paul makes it clear that, while these local or cultural issues may have provided the *context* of the issue, they do not provide the *reason* for his advice."[79] That reason is the "created role relationship of man and woman."[80] Since that reason is an abiding one, Paul's prohibitions apply to the church in every age.

Paul, we need to stress, is not forbidding women from teaching and from exercising authority in the church because the female gender is said to be inherently more gullible and prone to deception than men. Paul says nothing of the sort. Paul points to two events in history—the priority of Adam's creation to Eve's creation, and Eve's deception by the serpent and her consequent sin. These events—the role relationship of men and women divinely instituted at the creation, and Eve's violation of that order by her transgression—are the basis for God restricting the title and exercise of the office of elder in the church to men only.

Paul concludes this passage with the counsel to women that they "will be saved through childbearing—if they continue in faith and love and holiness, with self-control" (2:15). Likely Paul is giving a positive encouragement to Christian women to pursue the calling that God assigns them.

> Covenant women are saved in their God-given, created roles as mothers in the tradition of Sarah, Elizabeth, and Mary (cf. 1 Peter 3:5, 6). The curse for which she was partly responsible, by failing to submit to her husband's authority, is lifted in God's gracious salvation. Now by recalling to her God-given role as a suitable helper in the Covenant task, the Lord promises to save her as she trusts and obeys.[81]

Paul is not saying that women will save themselves by the good work of childbearing. Paul is saying to women, "Do not be distracted by the

79. Douglas Moo, "What Does It Mean Not to Teach or Have Authority Over Men?: 1 Timothy 2:11–15," in *Recovering Biblical Manhood and Womanhood: A Response to Evangelical Feminism*, ed. John Piper and Wayne Grudem (Wheaton, IL: Crossway, 1991), 190.

80. Ibid.

81. "Report of the Committee on Women in Church Office," 350.

pursuit of a task to which God has not called you. Pursue rather the noble and high calling to which God has called you. If you do, then you will have the assurance that the Lord is indeed your Savior." Redemption, Paul stresses, preserves, upholds, and restores the order that God established at the creation. Believers are to follow Christ and to grow in godliness precisely as they take up their creational callings.

Deacon. A separate question is whether women may serve in the office of deacon. While faithful Reformed churches have univocally followed the Scriptures in limiting the office of elder to men only, there has not been comparable agreement concerning the office of deacon. A minority of well-respected Reformed theologians has understood the Scriptures to admit women to the diaconate.[82] Two texts in particular, Romans 16:1 and 1 Timothy 3:11, are cited as offering biblical warrant for female deacons.

In what follows, we will argue that Scripture does not give clear indication that the office of deacon is open to women. If that is the case, then we must conclude that the office of deacon, like the office of elder, is open to men only. Further, we will see that Scripture makes provision for godly women to assist the deacons in their diaconal labors.

Following Thomas Witherow, B. B. Warfield identified Romans 16:1 ("I commend to you our sister Phoebe, a servant of the church in Cenchreae") as the sole passage warranting "women-deacons in the New Testament."[83] For this interpretation to prove what is argued,

---

82. B. B. Warfield, "Presbyterian Deaconesses," *The Presbyterian Review* 10, 38 (1889): 283–93; Patrick Fairbairn, *The Pastoral Epistles* (Edinburgh: T&T Clark, 1874; repr., Carlisle, PA: Banner of Truth, 2002), 149–51; Witherow, *The Form of the Christian Temple*, 86–87; Killen speaks of an "order of deaconesses," *The Framework of the Church*, 308; McGill, *Church Government*, 378–401; Clowney, *The Church*, 231–35; Robert Strimple, "Report of the Minority of the Committee on Women in Church Office (OPC);" and James B. Hurley, *Man and Woman in Biblical Perspective* (Grand Rapids: Zondervan, 1981), 223–33.

More cautiously, Thomas Cary Johnson says of the 1879 addition to the PCUS *Book of Church Order* concerning female assistants to the deacons (an addition that made its way into the PCA's *Book of Church Order*, cf. *BCO* 9–7), "It [the PCUS *Book of Church Order*] recognizes at least *quasi* deaconesses, which is a step in the right direction. If women had always been accorded the privilege of so serving the church, there might be less of obnoxious womanism among the churches to-day." *A History of the Southern Presbyterian Church, With Appendix*, American Church History Series, vol. 11 (New York: The Christian Literature Co., 1894), 414.

83. Warfield, "Deaconesses," 283.

the word translated "servant" (Greek *diakonos*) must refer to the title or office of deacon. The difficulty with this argument is that the Greek word may be used of both officers and non-officers, and there is, furthermore, no clear contextual indication that the term here refers to an officer. Warfield argues that the context could not rule out "deaconess" as the translation of this word, and that patristic church practice suggests that the post-apostolic church understood the New Testament to warrant "deaconesses."[84] The problem here is that this argument does not show that Paul's statement in Romans 16:1 warrants deaconesses in the apostolic church. Whatever subsequent interpreters may or may not have concluded from their study of this text, the context of Romans 16 does not demand the interpretation for which Warfield argues.

What about 1 Timothy 3:11? "Their wives likewise must be dignified, not slanderers, but sober-minded, faithful in all things" (note the ESV marginal gloss, "Or *Wives*, or *Women*"). There is no question that Paul is, here, giving a list of qualifications for a certain group of women. Furthermore, these qualifications are given in the midst of a broader discussion of the diaconate (1 Tim. 3:8–13). Proponents of women in the diaconate plausibly appeal to this passage to warrant some kind of inclusion of women in the diaconate.

There is no dispute that Paul describes the qualifications of male deacons at 1 Timothy 3:8–10, 12–13. The question concerns to what group of women Paul is referring at 1 Timothy 3:11. The word that Paul uses (*gynaikas*) may be translated either "wives" or "women." Many translations include the possessive pronoun "their," but there is no corresponding possessive in the Greek text. Is Paul referring, then, to the wives of the deacons (ESV), or to a separate group of women (ESV mg.)? If the latter, do these women hold, with men, the office of deacon? Do they occupy an office ("deaconess") that is the counterpart of the

84. Ibid., 284–86. Strimple offers more detailed exegetical argument, but the reservations I have expressed above apply *mutatis mutandis* to Strimple's discussion. It should also be stressed that the early church did not understand "deaconesses" to have "teaching authority" in the church; see Wayne Grudem, *Evangelical Feminism and Biblical Truth* (Sisters, OR: Multnomah, 2004), 266–68.

male-only office of deacon? Or, are they non-officer female assistants to the diaconate?[85]

There are several difficulties with understanding the women of verse 11 to refer to office-holders. First, Paul uses no title to refer to an office, "deaconess," in this passage. He simply refers to them as "wives" or "women." Second, whereas Paul stresses that a requirement for the office of both elder and deacon is that the candidate be "husband of one wife" (1 Tim. 3:2, 12), he gives no such matrimonial qualification here.[86] The absence of such a qualification suggests that Paul does not have a distinct office in mind at verse 11. Third, whereas Paul makes express provision for the testing of both deacons (1 Tim. 3:10) and elders (1 Tim. 5:22), he makes no such provision for the individuals in verse 11. Again, the absence of such a provision suggests that Paul is not thinking of an office or officers here. Fourth, verses 12–13 resume the qualifications of deacons that Paul had been discussing in verses 8–10. Verse 11 is something of a parenthesis to the discussion. When Paul discusses the offices of elder and deacon, however, he gives them discrete treatment. This format suggests that verse 11 does not introduce a new office into the discussion.

Finally, Paul expressly points to the candidate's management of his household as a qualification for the office of elder (3:5) and of deacon (3:12). In each case, Paul envisions a man overseeing his household. Capable leadership in the home qualifies him for leadership in the church, whether as elder or deacon. Even though the office of deacon is an "office of service" and not an "office of rule," it nevertheless is an office. The title and exercise of office in the church, Paul is saying, necessarily entails the possession and exercise of authority. The prohibition of women to the office of elder at 1 Timothy 2:12 therefore extends, in this respect, to the office of

85. These are the four exegetical possibilities proposed by George W. Knight III, "The Role of Women in the Church," in *Confessing Our Hope: Essays Celebrating the Life and Ministry of Morton H. Smith*. ed. Joseph A. Pipa Jr. and C. N. Willborn (Taylors, SC: Southern Presbyterian Press, 2004), 200.

86. Likely, Paul means to say that the candidate is sexually faithful to his spouse, with whom he is united in monogamous matrimony. Knight, *The Pastoral Epistles*, 158–59.

deacon.[87] This understanding of office is reflected, for instance, in the polity of the PCA.[88]

Individuals who understand Paul to be speaking of a distinct office at verse 11 raise an understandable objection to what we have been arguing. They might say, "First Timothy 3:11 gives positive indication that Paul has in mind a separate office of deaconess. After all, the word 'likewise' followed by a separate list of qualifications is precisely how Paul introduces the office of deacon, and distinguishes the office of deacon (3:7f.) from the office of elder (3:1–6)." We have above indicated several reasons why the text of verse 11 does not point to a separate office. The objection, nevertheless, raises good questions. For what purpose does Paul single this group of women out in the way that he does? Why does he not so speak of women in connection with his discussion of the eldership in 1 Timothy 3:1–6? One way to answer these questions is to reflect on what we have seen regarding the work of the deacon. Paul surely anticipated, as he goes on to say in 1 Timothy 5, that diaconal ministry would involve the deacons intimately in the lives of female members of the congregation. Propriety dictates that qualified women be available to assist the deacons in such labors, and who better to assist them than either their own wives[89] or suitable female assistants?[90] It is for

87. Appendix to the "Report of the Committee on Women in Church Office," 353.

88. See the PCA's *Book of Church Order*, 7–2, 3; 9–3; 24–1. Note the congregational vow on the occasion of the ordination of a deacon at 24–6: "Do you, the members of this church, acknowledge and receive this brother as a ruling elder (or deacon), and do you promise to yield to him all that honor, encouragement, and *obedience* in the Lord to which his office, according to the Word of God and the Constitution of this Church, entitles him?" (emphasis added). Compare the OPC's *Book of Church Order*, 5:2, 25:6.c., 6.e., 7.c., referenced in the Appendix to the "Report of the Committee of Women in the Church," 353.

89. Following ESV, "their wives," or ESV mg. "wives." Knight observes that the word *gyne* used at verse 12 means "wife" in the two other places Paul uses this word in 1 Tim. 3:1–13, i.e., verses 2 and 12. He also argues that "both the omission of the marital qualification of the wives in verse 11 and the placement of them before the marital qualification of the deacons are explained by the fact that they are wives of the deacons. That is, the marital status of their husbands is also their marital status and this status does not need to be repeated. They are mentioned at this juncture in their husbands' qualifications because they come at the beginning of a statement about a deacon's family life." Knight, "Role of Women in the Church," 200–201.

90. Following ESV mg., "women." This interpretation would certainly provide exegetical support to *BCO* 9–7, which permits the session to select and appoint godly women to assist the deacons in their diaconal labors.

this reason that Paul establishes a list of qualifications for such women in verse 11. This list, then, appropriately falls within Paul's discussion of the diaconate in 1 Timothy 3:8–13.

Positively, then, Paul is stressing that some women do have a critical role in the diaconal ministry of the church. The fact that Scripture does not call them to do this work as officers of the church in no way diminishes the privilege and value that Scripture assigns to this service. Here, as elsewhere in Scripture, God esteems and honors the service and contributions of women to the church.

In conclusion, the New Testament informs us that there are two and only two permanent offices in the church, elder and deacon. We have considered some of the important lines of biblical teaching concerning the eldership and the diaconate. We have also seen hints that elders and deacons serve the church at a level higher than that of the congregation. This breadth of service suggests an important point about the government of the church, namely, that it is not contained entirely within the local church. It is to this subject that we will turn in the next chapter.

5

THE COURTS OF THE CHURCH

I n the United States, government exists at several levels. There is government at the local level: districts, towns, and counties. Then, there is government at the state level. Finally, there is government at the federal level. Each level of government has certain defined responsibilities toward the citizens that it serves. Each level of government has constitutionally defined parameters within which it is supposed to operate. The actions and decisions of lower levels of government are subject to the supervision of higher levels of government. In this fashion, the government of the United States uniquely realizes and gives expression to the unity of the American nations.

Or, consider your family. On a day-to-day basis, you, your spouse, and your children interact with one another in countless ways. Although this phrase is not as common today, older Christian writers used to speak of "family government."[1] When we speak of family government, we mean to say that there is a relationship of "governor" and "governed" within the home.[2] Scripture calls fathers to exercise a God-appointed servant

1. A classic nineteenth-century treatment is that of B. M. Palmer, *The Family in Its Civil and Churchly Aspects: An Essay, In Two Parts* (Richmond, VA: Presbyterian Committee of Publication, 1876).

2. See Richard Baxter, "General Directions for the Holy Government of Families," in *Baxter's Practical Works*, vol. 1: *Christian Directory* (repr., Morgan, PA: Soli Deo Gloria, 1996), 422–24.

leadership in the home for the peace, flourishing, and well-being of his wife and children. Godly family government is characterized by love not bitterness; order not disorder; harmony not strife.

Now, consider your broader family. You have cousins, aunts and uncles, nieces and nephews, parents, or grandparents. Even though you no longer live with or even live near your parents, they are still your parents. Now that you have your own family, you are not under your parents' authority in the way that you were when you were a child. Even so, you have a biblical obligation to "honor your father and mother" (Exod. 20:12). You continue to receive the advice and counsel of your parents. Sometimes older parents prevail upon their sons to defer to their wisdom in matters that concern family government. These instances serve as reminders that your immediate household is part of a larger family and benefits from the wisdom and leadership of members of that larger family.

These examples from the family and from the state pose a question for our understanding of the church. If the church, like the family and state, has a government to "promote" the "fellowship" of its members, and if Scripture tells us that the church is broader and larger than the local congregation, then does Scripture also tell us that the church's government extends beyond and above the local congregation?[3]

In this chapter, we will argue that Scripture teaches that the church's government does in fact extend beyond and above the local congregation. We will furthermore consider the nature, composition, and responsibilities of that government. We will then take up the way in which the various levels of church government are to relate and interact with one another.

CHURCH GOVERNMENT—FOR THE WHOLE CHURCH

It is important to clarify what it is for which we are arguing. Where, for instance, do Presbyterians and Congregationalists agree?[4] Where do they differ?

3. Thomas E. Peck, *Notes on Ecclesiology* (Richmond, VA: Presbyterian Committee of Publication, 1892; repr., Greenville, SC: Presbyterian Press, 2005), 196.
4. I am using the term "Congregationalist" broadly to refer to individuals who understand the government of the church to extend no further than the local congregation. In doing so, I

Presbyterians and Congregationalists agree that the New Testament teaches the existence of what has been called the "invisible church." We considered this term in chapter 1. The invisible church, as the Westminster Larger Catechism defines it, is "the whole number of the elect that have been, are, or shall be gathered into one under Christ the head."[5] We see the invisible church reflected in such passages as Ephesians 5:25–27, where the apostle Paul tells us that "Christ loved the church and gave himself up for her, that he might sanctify her, having cleansed her by the washing of water with the word, so that he might present the church to himself in splendor, without spot or wrinkle or any such thing, that she might be holy and without blemish." There is no disagreement that the church, in this sense, exists beyond the level of the local congregation.

The disagreement concerns whether the visible church is to be governed at levels beyond the local congregation. Presbyterians argue in the affirmative, Congregationalists in the negative. Congregational church government does not deny that elders serving congregations may or even ought to convene for purposes of instruction, edification, and cooperative endeavor. These assemblies, however, are advisory but not governmental. They have no power to enforce their findings and actions with respect to local church membership. Properly speaking, church power is exercised only within the local congregation.

Presbyterianism argues that "Jesus Christ our Mediator has laid down in his Word a pattern of a Presbytery, and of one Presbyterial government in common over several single Congregations in one Church, for a rule to his Church in all later ages."[6] In other words, Presbyterians argue two related points. First, church government exists beyond the local level, and above the local congregation. Second, the

---

am passing over the historical differences between "congregationalism" and "independency," on which see James Bannerman, *The Church of Christ: A Treatise on the Nature, Powers, Ordinances, Discipline and Government of the Christian Church*, 2 vols. (London: Banner of Truth Trust, 1960), 2:296–300.

5. WLC 64.

6. *Jus Divinum Regiminis Ecclesiastici, or The Divine Right of Church-Government, originally asserted by the Ministers of Sion College, London, December, 1646* (1646; repr., rev. and ed., David Hall; Dallas, TX: Naphtali, 1995), 200.

local congregation therefore exists in a relationship of mutual account-ability and submission with other local congregations.

What is the evidence from Scripture for Presbyterian church govern-ment? Following Peck, we may point to three broad and related lines of biblical evidence. First, Scripture teaches the "unity of the church, even as a visible church catholic."[7] It is not simply that the church's unity exists with respect to the invisible church. It is that Scripture calls the visible church to give expression to a unity that belongs to the church. We see this teaching reflected in several passages.

> The glory that you have given me I have given to them, that they may be one even as we are one, I in them and you in me, that they may become perfectly one, so that the world may know that you sent me and loved them even as you loved me. (John 17:22–23)

> There is one body and one Spirit—just as you were called to the one hope that belongs to your call—one Lord, one faith, one baptism, one God and Father of all, who is over all and through all and in all. (Eph. 4:4–6)

> Because there is one bread, we who are many are one body, for we all partake of the one bread. (1 Cor. 10:17)

> For just as the body is one and has many members, and all the mem-bers of the body, though many, are one body, so it is with Christ. (1 Cor. 12:12)[8]

It is impossible to restrict the unity in view in these passages to that of the local congregation. Jesus and Paul teach that there is a unity that belongs to the visible church as a whole.[9] This unity is reflected in the

---

7. Peck, *Notes on Ecclesiology*, 195.

8. Ibid. Peck, in turn, quotes these texts from John M. Mason, *Essays on the Church of God: In Which the Doctrines of Church Membership and Infant Baptism Are Fully Discussed* (1843; repr., Taylors, SC: Presbyterian Press, 2005).

9. It is in light of this truth that the PCA's *BCO* says, "This visible unity of the body of Christ, though obscured, is not destroyed by its division into different denominations of profess-

biblical account of the growth and progress of the early church. In Acts 9:31, Luke comments parenthetically, after the conversion of Saul to Christianity, "So the church throughout all Judea and Galilee and Samaria had peace and was being built up. And walking in the fear of the Lord and in the comfort of the Holy Spirit, it multiplied." Scripture, then, can speak of a sizable portion of the people of God spread over a wide geographical region as "the church" (singular).

It is one thing for the visible church to possess and to express unity. It is another for this unity to "warrant the union of two or more congregations in the same government."[10] Does the unity of the church entail such a government?

This brings us to our second point: during the apostolic period, the church existed in several congregations. Scripture speaks of these congregations collectively as the "church," and understands those congregations to be united in one government. Two further points will bear this observation out.[11] The first is that the Acts of the Apostles more than once describes the church in Jerusalem using the word "church" in the singular.

> And there arose on that day a great persecution against the church in Jerusalem. (Acts 8:1)

> The report of this came to the ears of the church in Jerusalem, and they sent Barnabas to Antioch. (Acts 11:22)

> When they came to Jerusalem, they were welcomed by the church and the apostles and the elders. (Acts 15:4)

Scripture, then, speaks of all the believers in Jerusalem as "the church." Second, "the church at Jerusalem must have consisted of several

---

ing Christians; but all of these which maintain the Word and Sacraments in their fundamental integrity are to be recognized as true branches of the Church of Jesus Christ." *BCO* 2–2.

10. Peck, *Notes on Ecclesiology*, 196.

11. What follows is heavily indebted to Peck, *Notes on Ecclesiology*, 200–201. A fuller and more detailed version of the type of argument Peck makes may be found at *Jus Divinum*, 201–16. What we argue here of the church in Jerusalem the authors of *Jus Divinum* also argue of the church in Antioch, Ephesus, and Corinth.

congregations."[12] The Acts of the Apostles records steady and substantial numerical growth in the church at Jerusalem. The church began with 120 disciples and, by the Lord's grace, grew exponentially.

> So those who received his word were baptized, and there were added that day about three thousand souls. (Acts 2:41)

> And the Lord added to their number day by day those who were being saved. (Acts 2:47)

> But many of those who had heard the word believed, and the number of the men came to about five thousand. (Acts 4:4)

> And more than ever believers were added to the Lord, multitudes of both men and women. (Acts 5:14)

> And the word of God continued to increase, and the number of disciples multiplied greatly in Jerusalem, and a great many of the priests became obedient to the faith. (Acts 6:7)

> And [James and all the elders (in Jerusalem)] said to [Paul], "You see, brother, how many thousands there are among the Jews of those who have believed." (Acts 21:20).

To be sure, these passages are attended with a number of exegetical difficulties.[13] The main thrust of Luke's description, however, should

12. Peck, *Notes on Ecclesiology*, 200.

13. For instance, does the number of believers given in Acts 4:4 include the number given in Acts 2:41, or is Luke saying that 5,000 believers (Acts 4:4) were added to the already existing 3,000 believers (Acts 2:41)? For discussion, see J. A. Alexander, *A Commentary on the Acts of the Apostles,* 2 vols. (New York: Charles Scribner, 1857; repr., Edinburgh: Banner of Truth, 1963), 1:129–31. Furthermore, it is not altogether clear that the numbers given in Acts always reflect the church in Jerusalem as such. Some or many of these individuals may have left Jerusalem for other parts of Palestine or for the Diaspora lands. On this question, see D. Douglas Bannerman, *The Scripture Doctrine of the Church: Historically and Exegetically Considered* (1887; repr., Grand Rapids: Baker, 1976), 396–99. Interestingly, these concerns (and more) were raised and addressed by the authors of *Jus Divinum,* 206–10.

not be lost on the reader. As J. A. Alexander notes, "Even on the lowest computation of the numbers in the case before us [i.e., that of Acts 4:4], the increase of the Church was wonderfully great and rapid."[14] A conservative estimate would place the membership of the church at Jerusalem at the close of the Acts of the Apostles at not fewer than several thousand persons.

The Jerusalem believers must have gathered in separate congregations. These were the days before stadium-sized congregations. The testimony of Scripture and subsequent church history is that public meeting places dedicated for ecclesiastical uses were a post-New Testament phenomenon. Meeting places for the church, Acts and the Epistles tell us, were private dwellings (Acts 1:12–14; 2:46; 12:12; 19:9; 20:8; 28:30–31; Rom. 16:5; 1 Cor. 16:19; Col. 4:15; Philem. 2).[15] The fact that thousands of believers met in individual homes necessarily leads one to the conclusion that the church in Jerusalem gathered in several congregations.[16]

These Jerusalem believers were served by several officers. We read, of course, of the ministry of the twelve apostles throughout the opening chapters of Acts. We have witnessed the institution of the diaconate in Acts 6:1–6. We also learn that the church in Jerusalem was served by elders alongside the apostles (Acts 15:2). This multiplicity of church officers suits a church gathered in separate congregations. It is reasonable to conclude that these congregations were collectively governed by the apostles; and individually governed by groups of elders chosen by the congregation to serve the congregation (see Acts 6:1–6).[17]

We have observed above that these congregations were properly termed a single church (Acts 8:1). We also see that this regional church is "represented as acting in concert" through her officers in matters of church government.[18] Three passages of Scripture help us to see this

14. Alexander, *Commentary on Acts*, 1:131.

15. *Jus Divinum*, 211.

16. This is precisely the pattern of the synagogue in Jerusalem. See now the discussion at Lee I. Levine, *The Ancient Synagogue: The First Thousand Years,* 2nd ed. (New Haven, CT: Yale University Press, 2005).

17. As Peck notes, "Each [apostle] was a governor of the whole church . . . from the very nature of the apostolic office." *Notes on Ecclesiology*, 201.

18. Ibid.

regional church government. In Acts 11:22, we see the elders of the church in Jerusalem sending Barnabas to encourage and to serve the church at Antioch. In Acts 11:30, we see the elders receiving and, by implication, disbursing the relief fund sent by the Antiochene believers to the church in Jerusalem. In Acts 15:2, we see the elders of the church in Jerusalem receiving Paul and Barnabas to begin discussing and deliberating upon a question of doctrine and practice.[19]

We may speak, then, of the church at both the local and the regional levels. At each level, she is governed by a plurality of elders. At the local level, the congregation is governed by elders whom that congregation has chosen to serve her. At a broader or higher level, the church is governed by a representation of the elders within a particular region.[20]

From this observation, we may draw the conclusion that the visible church, at her highest or broadest extent, is to be governed by representation of her elders. What the data of Acts show us is that the church's government extends as highly and as broadly as the visible church extends. If the visible church is universal, it stands to reason that Scripture calls the church to be governed at that level by a representation of the whole church's elders.

It is important to see that, biblically, the existence of the church locally in several congregations in no way delimits or is set against her identity and work as the church more broadly. In fact, as Peck observes, it is "Presbyterian church government" that "realizes the unity of the church" by the "*elasticity* of its parliamentary representative system."[21]

> If there was but one congregation on earth, its presbytery or "session," would constitute the parliament of the whole church; if half-a-dozen, the representatives from each would constitute a parliament for the whole church; if a still larger number, the same results would follow. And representatives from all the churches (or from the smaller parliaments, which is the same principle,) constitute the parliament for the whole church. . . . Presbyterianism may, therefore, be thus defined: The government of the church by parliamentary assemblies, composed

19. These three examples are drawn from *Jus Divinum*, 217–18.
20. We will discuss below the representative character of the higher courts of the church.
21. Peck, *Notes on Ecclesiology*, 203; emphasis Peck's.

of two classes of presbyters, and of presbyters only, and so arranged as to realize the visible unity of the whole church.[22]

This "elasticity" affords the church flexibility in bringing to expression her unity.

> The arrangement of the courts, their number, extent of territory, etc., is an affair to be determined by human wisdom, accommodating its plans to the circumstances of the case, with a view to decency, order, and general edification. Mountains, rivers, political divisions, language and other circumstances do and must modify our attempts to realize, in any external form, the idea of the unity of the church.[23]

"Divine Right" Presbyterianism, therefore, is remarkably adapted both to the exigencies of an expanding church and to the realization of the unity of the church in every age. As the church grows, the government that Christ has given to the church may grow with it. The church may be confident that she will encounter no set of circumstances that will require her to jettison or to modify her form of government. Surely this state of affairs is a testimony to the wisdom of Christ, the head of the church.

Before we proceed, it is worth stressing that we advance this argument for Presbyterianism with modest certainty. As Peck notes, this reflection has important implications for our interactions with our non-Presbyterian brothers and sisters.

> Absolute certainty cannot be reached upon these points as it can be in regard to those articles of faith which are fundamental and necessary to salvation. And, hence, while we contend for the scriptural order of Christ's house, as a matter of faith and of vast importance to the prosperity and efficiency of the church, we do not unchurch and remit to the uncovenanted mercies of God those who, holding the head, yet differ from us upon these points.[24]

22. Ibid.
23. Ibid., 194.
24. Ibid., 202–3.

As we saw in the Introduction, Presbyterianism is essential to the well-being (*bene esse*) but not to the essence (*esse*) of the church. Non-acceptance of Presbyterianism is, therefore, no barrier to receiving a non-Presbyterian person as a Christian, or a non-Presbyterian church as a true branch of the church, provided that he in fact holds fast the only Head of the church, Jesus Christ.

THE ASSEMBLIES OF THE CHURCH

So far, we have argued two fundamental points in this chapter. First, Scripture acknowledges that the visible church is broader and higher than the local congregation. We may properly speak of all true congregations in a region, in fact all true congregations on the planet, as "the church." Second, Scripture represents congregations as "connected together in government."[25] The church has government at the local level, to be sure, but she also has government at higher levels. Let us now consider what form church government takes at these higher levels.

Before we take up this matter, let us review what we have concluded regarding church government at the local level. We have seen that congregations are governed by a plurality of elders (Acts 14:23; Phil. 1:1; Titus 1:5). Presbyterians often call this gathering of elders a "session."[26] The "session" might properly be termed a "presbytery," since a "presbytery" in its most general sense is a college of elders.[27] Presbyterians, however, tend to reserve the term "presbytery" to describe the regional church, which also meets as a court of the church.[28]

The session is an example of a church court. The term "court" refers to the elders gathering together in order to declare the law of God for the benefit of the church. The session has responsibilities that fall over three areas that we considered in chapter 3: doctrine, order, and jurisdiction.

25. Ibid., 194.
26. From a Latin word meaning "to sit," i.e., in deliberation and judgment.
27. Peck, *Notes on Ecclesiology*, 191. For discussion of the Greek term *presbyterion*, see Knight, *The Pastoral Epistles*, 209.
28. "The Presbytery consists of all the teaching elders and churches within its bounds that have been accepted by the Presbytery. When the Presbytery meets as a court it shall comprise all teaching elders and ruling elders as elected by their Session." *BCO* 13–1.

In chapter 4, we gave attention to one such responsibility of a church court, namely, the ordination of men to church office.

Sessions are comprised both of teaching elders and ruling elders. Since teaching elders and ruling elders are two distinct orders within the same office, and since Scripture appoints no hierarchical structure within the eldership or over the eldership, the courts must act through "deliberation, conference, interchange of views, and a [majority] vote which makes the action of the whole governing body."[29]

If sessions have such a composition and character, what may we say of the character and composition of the higher or broader courts of the church? What may we say of the presbytery (the regional church) when it meets as a court? What may we say of the General Assembly, which "is the highest court of [the] church, and represents in one body all the churches thereof"?[30] Thankfully, Scripture furnishes an example of the workings of a higher court in Acts 15.[31] Let us turn to this chapter and see what principles we can learn about the government of the church at the level of the presbytery and the General Assembly.[32]

Five observations are pertinent to our concern. The first has to do with the composition of the Jerusalem Council. The assembly of Acts 15 is a representative assembly. It is composed of representatives sent by several churches, as we see in Acts 15:2: "Paul and Barnabas and some of the others were appointed to go up to Jerusalem to the apostles and the elders about this question." Scripture tells us that these representatives are "appointed" by the church to serve in Jerusalem. Because this appointment is an act of government, we may conclude

29. Peck, *Notes on Ecclesiology*, 189. It is because of this character of the church court as a deliberative assembly that many such courts adopt such standards of parliamentary procedure as *Robert's Rules of Order, Newly Revised*.

30. *BCO* 14–1.

31. We have seen that the church in Jerusalem was likely composed of several congregations joined together in a single government. This is likely true of other regions where the church was present during the apostolic period. The Council recorded in Acts 15, then, is a court of the universal church or, at a minimum, of several regional churches.

32. The following discussion is indebted to William Cunningham, *Historical Theology: A Review of the Principal Doctrinal Discussions in the Christian Church Since the Apostolic Age*, 2 vols. (1870; repr. London: Banner of Truth Trust, 1960), 1:43–78, and *Jus Divinum*, 225–36.

that it was the elders of the church at Antioch that acted in selecting Paul and Barnabas.

Furthermore, the representatives to the Jerusalem Council are all apostles or elders. Not fewer than five times in this account Luke reminds his readers that it was the "apostles and the elders" who were the participants in the Jerusalem Council (15:4, 6, 22, 23; 16:4). As Acts 15:6 ("The apostles and the elders were gathered together to consider this matter") and Acts 16:4 ("the decisions that had been reached by the apostles and elders who were in Jerusalem") make particularly clear, non-officers do not take part directly in the work of this assembly. Since the office of apostle is one that has ceased, the membership of such assemblies today is to consist exclusively of elders.

These elders, Scripture also informs us, are drawn from several congregations. The delegation of the church at Antioch is comprised of Paul and Barnabas (15:2), who join "the apostles and elders" in Jerusalem. Since the matter before the Council affected churches other than at Jerusalem and Antioch (see Acts 15:23), other unnamed churches presumably sent representatives as well.[33] This assembly, then, is a court not of the local church but of the broader church.

Acts shows us, then, that the higher courts of the church are to be composed of elders. These elders are chosen by the lower courts of which they are part. The higher courts, furthermore, serve the broader church.

Some have argued that because several apostles are recorded as participants in this Assembly, the Assembly is not normative for subsequent church government. In other words, the apostles are said to have "acted *in this matter* as inspired and infallible expounders of the will of God."[34] On the contrary, we see the apostles Peter, Paul, Barnabas, and James participating in the work of the Council as "the ordinary

33. *Jus Divinum*, 228–29.
34. Cunningham, *Historical Theology*, 1:45. Cunningham is summarizing here a standard Congregational understanding of Acts 15. It is not only Congregationalists, however, who understand the chapter in this way. See Alexander, *Commentary on Acts*, 2:92. Peck reports that this position was also Thornwell's view. Thomas E. Peck, "The Action of the Assembly of 1879 on Worldly Amusements, or The Powers of Our Several Church Courts," in *Miscellanies of Thomas E. Peck,* 3 vols. (Richmond, VA: Presbyterian Committee of Publication, 1895–97; repr., Edinburgh: Banner of Truth, 1999), 2:351.

office-bearers of the church, using the ordinary means of ascertaining the divine will, and enjoying only the ordinary guidance and influences of His Spirit."[35] We never see the apostles in the Council invoking their apostolic authority. Rather, they participate as elders with other elders in the process of deliberation. The Council's conclusion, Scripture tells us, is owing to a consensus forged through debate, not the invocation of infallible apostolic judgment. The apostles were certainly entitled to conclude the matter in this way. They opted, however, not to act here as "inspired and infallible expounders of the will of God."[36] They chose to act as "fellow elder[s]" (1 Peter 5:1). In so doing, they show us that Scripture intends this Council and its workings to be regulative of the church's practice in every age.

The second observation concerns the matter that the Council addresses. Luke specifies the issue for us at Acts 15:1: "Some men came down from Judea and were teaching the brothers, 'Unless you are circumcised according to the custom of Moses you cannot be saved.'" The matter is a specifically ecclesiastical concern and involves a corruption of the gospel. This is the kind of matter that properly comes before a court of the church of Jesus Christ.

What's more, this matter had been the occasion of "dissension and debate" in the church at Antioch. It had apparently troubled the church in Syria and Cilicia as well (15:23). This concern was not restricted to a single congregation or even to a specific regional church but was impacting the church more broadly. The seriousness and widespread character of this matter therefore warranted the consideration of a higher court of the church.

Notice, furthermore, how the matter comes to the attention of the Council. The matter comes by reference of the church of Antioch to a higher court of the church.[37] This course of action was not the only one available to the Antiochene church, as William Cunningham explains.

---

35. Cunningham, *Historical Theology*, 1:45. Cunningham here offers a standard Presbyterian understanding of Acts 15. See his discussion of this point at *Historical Theology*, 1:45–47; cf. *Jus Divinum*, 229–31.

36. Using Cunningham's phrase. *Historical Theology*, 1:45.

37. Cunningham, *Historical Theology*, 1:59.

It is plain that, if the church at Antioch, instead of referring the matter to the church at Jerusalem, had themselves given a decision upon it, as they might have done, it would have been equally competent for the minority in the church at Antioch (for we know there was a division there) to have appealed to the church at Jerusalem to review, and, if they saw cause, to reverse the decision.[38]

The Jerusalem Council, then, illustrates an important principle for church government. Higher courts have a supervisory role with respect to the lower courts of the church. Whether this concern had come to the Council by complaint or, as it actually did, by reference, this Council had authority to act upon matters that were constitutionally brought before it by a lower court.[39] We will consider below what authority any decisions of the higher courts carry with respect to the lower courts of the church in particular and to the church in general.

The third observation concerns the manner in which the Council addressed the matter brought to it by the church in Antioch.[40] It did so through deliberation. What is the character of this deliberation? We may note two principal characteristics. First, we see that the participant elders engage one another as equals. The discussion affords no evidence that any one individual possesses or exercises hierarchical authority over others.

Second, the deliberation is orderly and rational, and proceeds along premises drawn from Scripture. It is orderly. Each person speaks in turn. It is rational. Each person's contribution builds upon and does not merely restate what the previous person has just said. It is biblical. The deliberation is preeminently concerned to bring Scripture to bear on the matter before the Council.[41] Peter, Paul, and Barnabas relate the

38. Ibid., 1:60.
39. See this principle articulated and developed at *BCO* 39–1, 2, 3.
40. For what follows, I am particularly indebted to David F. Coffin Jr.
41. Cunningham notes that the Council appeals to both the providence of God and the Scriptures. He carefully observes, however, that "the written word of God is, properly speaking, the only standard by which the affairs of the church ought to be regulated, though much is to be learned from carefully considering His providence, or what He has actually done, in connection with the statements of His word." *Historical Theology*, 1:48.

THE COURTS OF THE CHURCH

activity of God in connection with their ministry to the Gentiles. We have an inspired account of this activity in Acts 10–11 and Acts 13–14. James quotes the prophet Amos in reference to the situation facing the Council, and proceeds to draw from the prophet practical conclusions for the Council to follow (see Acts 15:15–21).

The fourth observation concerns the nature and authority of the decision of the Council. The elders present in Jerusalem do not deliberate for the sake of deliberation. They deliberate in order to reach a conclusion. The Council ultimately takes three courses of action.[42] They reach a decision, they draft their decision in an explanatory letter to be distributed to the broader church, and they select men to bear this letter personally to the various churches represented at the Council.

What may we say of the conclusion itself? Formally, just as the deliberation proceeded along biblical premises, the conclusion that logically follows from these premises is biblical as well. The Council tells the church that it understands its decision to be biblical by introducing it thus: "it seemed good to the Holy Spirit and to us" (15:28).[43] The Council, then, shows us that "all the decrees and determinations of Councils or Church Courts should be regulated by the word of God."[44]

Materially, the Council's conclusion demonstrates both the dogmatic and the diatactical power of a court of the church. Its dogmatic power is seen in the Assembly's resolution of the doctrinal matter brought before it by the church in Antioch.[45] The Council does so when it says that "some persons have gone out from us and troubled you with

42. *Jus Divinum*, 231.

43. "This statement certainly implies that they were confident that the decision was *de facto* in accordance with the mind of the Holy Ghost. . . . Christ, the Head of the church, determined the disposal of this matter, not by direct and infallible inspiration, but by a general meeting of apostles and elders seeking and attaining the truth upon the point, by means accessible to men in general with the ordinary influences of the Spirit." Cunningham, *Historical Theology*, 1:46.

44. Cunningham, *Historical Theology*, 1:53.

45. Significantly, the Assembly refrains from passing judicial sentence on the individuals who were teaching this false doctrine. Likely this is because a judicial appeal had not properly come before the Assembly concerning a case first adjudicated by a lower court. The Assembly, rather, limits itself to addressing the doctrinal merits of the teaching in question, as well as acknowledging some of the practical consequences of that teaching. See Peck, "Worldly Amusements," in *Miscellanies*, 2:355.

words, unsettling your minds, although we gave them no instructions" (15:24), and when it makes provision for Judas and Silas to confirm the same personally before the churches (15:27). The Assembly, in other words, upholds the doctrine of justification by faith alone and expressly disavows a doctrine of justification by works that is circulating among the churches.[46]

The Assembly exercises diatactical power, or the power of order, when it says to the churches that they ought to refrain from certain matters.

> For it has seemed good to the Holy Spirit and to us to lay on you no greater burden than these requirements: that you abstain from what has been sacrificed to idols, and from blood, and from what has been strangled, and from sexual immorality. If you keep yourselves from these, you will do well. (Acts 15:28–29)

The Assembly highlights four matters of tremendous importance to Jews. The Assembly is not saying that these are the only matters of behavior about which the first-century Christians should have been concerned. Nor are they saying that each is as morally important as the other. They are, rather, pointing believers to these four matters for a specific reason. Having affirmed the doctrinal point that the believer is justified by faith alone and not by works of the law, and that believers under the New Covenant are not bound to be circumcised, the Assembly is concerned that this doctrine not give unnecessary offense. Although three of these four matters concern "things indifferent" for the believer, the Assembly urges believers nevertheless to observe them, and to do so for the sake of avoiding needless offense, whether of weaker believing Jews or of unbelieving Jews. For this reason, the Assembly is not exercising legislative power. The Assembly, rather, is exercising the jurisdictional power of order. This court orders circumstances for the sake of the peace and unity of the church, and for the honor of the gospel.

This discussion raises two further questions. First, is this decree binding on believers today with respect to its counsel of abstaining from

46. *Jus Divinum*, 232.

"what has been sacrificed to idols, and from blood, and from what has been strangled"? The answer to this question is "no." The reason is because the circumstances that occasioned the church's exercise of the power of order in Jerusalem no longer exist today. It is highly unlikely that my purchasing at the grocery store a package of hamburger meat with a little blood still in the package will offend my neighbor or fellow church member because of reasons relating to the ceremonial laws of Moses.

Second, would it have been a sin for a Christian in the first-century Jerusalem church to eat meat sacrificed to idols in defiance of the decree? The answer to this question is a qualified "yes." To have done so would have been sin, but the sin would not have been in the eating of the meat itself. Were this the case, we would have to acknowledge the power of the Assembly to legislate a matter not legislated by Scripture. The Assembly, after all, recognized that New Covenant believers were free from such ceremonial obligations. The sin, rather, would have consisted in the scandal brought by this action. Consequently, "the discipline is administered for the scandal rather than for the violation of the rule itself."[47]

What may we say of the authority of the decision of the Council? Scripture indicates that the Assembly's conclusions were not advisory in nature. The decision was "an authoritative judgment."[48] We read in Acts 15:28 that the Assembly is laying a "burden" upon the church in Antioch, Syria, and Cilicia. Furthermore, when Paul and Silas deliver the Assembly's work to the church, Luke tells us that "they delivered to them for observance the decisions that had been reached by the apostles and elders who were in Jerusalem" (Acts 16:4). The fact that the Assembly's deliverance had an authoritative character and was imposed upon the lower courts of the church shows us an important principle of biblical church government, that of "the subordination of one court to another of wider jurisdiction—of the subordination of one church to many churches, or to their representatives."[49] We will consider below more closely this gradation of the courts of the church.

47. Peck, "Worldly Amusements," in *Miscellanies*, 2:356.
48. Cunningham, *Historical Theology*, 1:61. See also *Jus Divinum*, 233–34.
49. Cunningham, *Historical Theology*, 1:62. "A Synod or Council of which they were constituent members might be fairly regarded as representing the church, and as thus entitled

The fifth and final observation from Acts 15 concerns how the church receives the decisions of a higher court. We have already seen that the Jerusalem Council was composed exclusively of elders. The people play no part in the Council's deliberations.[50] This decision, however, is submitted to the consideration of the whole church in the form of the drafting and distribution of the Assembly's letter. What is the purpose of this submission?

We can say that the purpose was not to give the people an opportunity to veto or nullify the decision. Scripture gives no indication that the people have such authority. The purpose, rather, was to gain the "consent and concurrence" of the people.[51] This consent and concurrence is not an act of governance. Rather, it is an acknowledgment that the decision of the Assembly is what it professed to be—a decision consonant with Scripture. The Assembly takes care to demonstrate that its deliberations and conclusions were biblical because it wants the church to receive its judgments as such. We see here a further principle of biblical church government. It is not enough that a decision of a church court be biblical; it must also be *perceived* to be biblical. This desire shapes the way in which the Assembly both drafts and promulgates its actions.

Scripture therefore upholds what has been called the "right of private judgment," that is, that each Christian "is entitled to interpret the word of God for himself upon his own responsibility, for the regulation of his own opinions and conduct, for the execution of his own functions and the discharge of his own duties, *whatever these may be*."[52] The officers of the church do not stand between Christ and the conscience of the believer. On the contrary, Scripture in Acts 15 puts on vivid display the ministerial power that elders are called to exercise.

---

to exercise over the whole length and breadth of it whatever authority and jurisdiction was in itself right or competent." Ibid.

50. Even so, the decision of the court is said to be the judgment of the whole church (15:22), that is, the church working through her officers.

51. Cunningham, *Historical Theology*, 1:56.

52. Ibid., 1:51. See Cunningham's discussion for an elaboration of the critical distinction between the people having no authority to "interpret the word of God for the purpose of executing this function [of governance]," but inalienably retaining the right of private judgment in receiving the acts and deliverances of a court of the church. Ibid., 1:52.

Notice the results of the Council's actions in the church: "So the churches were strengthened in the faith, and they increased in numbers daily" (16:5). The action of the Assembly did not divide the church. Neither did it dampen or hamper the evangelistic work of the church. On the contrary, the action of the Assembly served to upbuild and to extend the church in at least two ways. First, the church was "strengthened in the faith." Imagine the relief that believers, beleaguered by false teaching within the church, experienced when they read this letter and heard men like Paul and Silas explaining it to them. Imagine their encouragement to have learned that the church had so reaffirmed her commitment to the gospel. When church government works properly, the church enjoys unity not fragmentation.

Second, the church "increased in numbers daily." This result should be no surprise to us. Believers united in and fortified by the gospel scattered to tell others the good news about Jesus. By the grace of God, sinners were brought to faith and repentance, made public profession of faith, and joined the fellowship of believers. This passage should help us to see that biblical church government is no obstacle to missions and evangelism. In fact, Scripture shows us that good church government is critical to the expansion of the church. After this Assembly has done its work, the church continues to grow by the Lord's blessing. Jesus, then, is blessing his own means to gather and to perfect the saints.

RECEIVING THE ACTIONS OF CHURCH COURTS TODAY

Christians have long recognized that the courts of the church are liable to err. No Protestant claims that church officers or church courts are infallible. The Westminster Confession of Faith correctly summarizes the teaching of Scripture when it says that "all synods or councils, since the apostles' times, whether general or particular, may err; and many have erred. Therefore they are not to be made the rule of faith, or practice; but to be used as a help in both."[53] Decisions of church courts,

53. WCF 31.3.

then, may only command the assent of the individual in so far as they are faithful to Scripture.

This point is so important that it forms the first of the Preliminary Principles to the PCA's *Book of Church Order*.

> God alone is Lord of the conscience and has left it free from any doctrines or commandments of men (a) which are in any respect contrary to the Word of God, or (b) which, in regard to matters of faith and worship, are not governed by the Word of God. Therefore the rights of private judgment in all matters that respect religion are universal and inalienable.

Scripture acknowledges both the universality and inalienability of the rights of private judgment in all matters that respect religion, and the fallibility of the courts of the church. This state of affairs permits the rise of a certain practical question—what am I to do when I am convinced that a court of the church has erred?

The Assembly of Acts 15 enjoyed, it appears, universal consensus with respect to its decision. There appears to have been no dissenting vote. But what happens when a church officer today finds himself at variance with a decision of a church court of which he is a member? What should he do? What should he not do? What are his obligations to Christ and to the church in such a situation? What principles should guide him in making these kinds of decisions? How do these principles, furthermore, help non-officers weigh the decisions of church courts?

To answer these questions, we may turn to an early chapter in American Presbyterian history. In 1741, the Presbyterian Church experienced a painful split and divided into two separate church bodies, the Synod of Philadelphia and the Synod of New York.[54] When these synods reunited in 1758, the new body, the Synod of New York and Philadel-

---

54. For an account of this "Old Side/New Side" split, see D. G. Hart and John R. Muether, *Seeking a Better Country: 300 Years of American Presbyterianism* (Phillipsburg, NJ: P&R Publishing, 2007), 50–69; Lefferts A. Loetscher, *A Brief History of the Presbyterians,* 4th ed. (Philadelphia: Westminster, 1983), 63–70.

phia, adopted a Plan of Union spelling out the "terms of reunion."[55] The reunited Synod's stated goal in drafting and adopting the plan was "that no jealousies or grounds of alienation may remain, and also to prevent future breaches of like nature."[56]

The first paragraph of the plan indicated that the reunited church bodies would continue to "approve and receive" the Westminster Standards, as well as the "plan of worship, government, and discipline, contained in the Westminster Directory."[57]

In the next two paragraphs, the Synod indicated the ways in which individual voting members could respond to decisions of the whole body.

> When any matter is determined by a major vote, every member shall either actively concur with, or passively submit to such determination; or, if his conscience permit him to do neither, he shall, after sufficient liberty modestly to reason and remonstrate, peaceably withdraw from our communion, without attempting to make any schism. Provided always, that this shall be understood to extend only to such determinations as the body shall judge indispensable in doctrine, or Presbyterian government.

> That any member or members, for the exoneration of his or their conscience before God, have a right to protest against any act or procedure of our highest judicature, because there is no further appeal to another for redress; and to require that such protestation be recorded in their minutes. And as such a protest is a solemn appeal from the bar of said judicature, no member is liable to persecution on the account of his protesting. Provided always, that it shall be deemed irregular and unlawful, to enter a protestation against any member or members, or to protest facts or accusations instead of proving them, unless a fair trial be refused, even by the highest judicature. And it

---

55. Hart and Muether, *Seeking a Better Country*, 67. For the authors' analysis of the Plan of Union, see 67–69.

56. *Records of the Presbyterian Church in the United States of America, 1706–1788* (1841; repr., New York: Arno Press & The New York Times, 1969), 286; Charles Hodge, *Constitutional History of the Presbyterian Church in the United States,* 2 vols. (Philadelphia: Presbyterian Board of Publication, 1851), 2:277.

57. *Records of the Presbyterian Church, 1706–1788*, 286.

is agreed, that protestations are only to be entered against the public acts, judgments, or determinations of the judicature with which the protester's conscience is offended.[58]

The Synod's principles admirably balance two important principles—the determination of a court's decision by majority vote, and the rights of minority members to give expression to and to act upon their convictions.

First, the Synod upholds the principle that a church court reaches its decisions by majority vote. We have earlier observed that this principle is required by two characteristics of church courts—the absence of any hierarchicalism within its membership, and the deliberative character of its proceedings. The Synod does not permit a minority to upset or to frustrate the decision of the majority. In so doing, order is preserved in the courts of the church.

Second, the Synod vindicates the rights of the minority to give expression to and to act upon its convictions. It does so by charting three possible courses of action for all members of the assembly. The first is active concurrence. When the member actively concurs with a matter determined by majority vote, he is in full agreement with and is willing to promote that matter.

What happens, however, when a member is unable actively to concur with this decision? In this case, two options are available to him. He may "passively submit." He is unable conscientiously to concur with the decision. At the same time, he is willing to let the matter rest, and to submit in this sense to the will of his brethren.

Or, the member may "peaceably withdraw" from the assembly. He is unable conscientiously to concur with the decision, and is unable otherwise to submit to the will of his brethren. If he withdraws, however, three conditions must be in place. First, he must have made the effort "modestly to reason and remonstrate" with his fellow elders. He has the right to appeal and even to protest without fear of prosecution for an appropriate protest. Second, the majority must judge its "determinations" to be "indispensable in doctrine, or Presbyterian government."

58. Ibid.; Hodge, *Constitutional History*, 2:277–78.

This provision ensures that, should the minority depart, the majority will not be guilty of unnecessarily dividing the body. This provision also gives the majority occasion to rethink whether it deems its decision to be of sufficient importance to press forward with it in the face of such minority dissent. Third, the minority may withdraw "without attempting to make any such schism." The provision helps the minority to be sure that he is acting for conscience's sake alone, and not for other, sinful purposes.

On the face of it, such processes could appear to be destructive of the church's unity. They may seem to aggravate tensions between the majority and the minority. In fact, these processes are designed to preserve and to promote church unity. By ensuring the majority's right to carry the assembly, and by limiting what the minority may and may not do after a matter has been carried, the Synod prevents a minority of the body from holding the whole body captive to its concerns. By ensuring the minority's right to give expression to and to act upon its convictions, the Synod places an obstacle to the formation of a false unity within the court that tramples upon the consciences of its membership. By permitting the minority to protest, the Synod encourages the majority to reconsider both the importance and the rightness of its action.

How might these principles work in practice? Let us look at a trivial and hypothetical example. Supposing the General Assembly of some Presbyterian church condemns, by majority vote, the purchase and consumption of pistachio ice cream. What is a member of the assembly to do? He may "actively concur" with the decision. He may think that it is biblically warranted for a court of the church to lay such a ban on pistachio ice cream. He may put his full support into working to encourage church members to put this decision into practice. Or, he may "passively submit" to the decision. He thinks that Scripture does not legislate flavors of ice cream, and, besides, that this is a matter to which a court of the church has no business speaking. Even so, his convictions are such that he is willing to pursue the matter no further.

Or, he may consider "peaceable withdrawal." To pursue this course of action, however, he must first "modestly . . . reason and remonstrate" with the brethren. He must work to show them that this judgment is both unbiblical in content and inappropriate for a court of the church to have rendered. He must do so with tempered, persuasive arguments. The majority must ask itself whether legislating ice cream is in fact so indispensable to biblical doctrine and church government that it is willing to press forward with the measure and to risk losing a member of the court. If the majority persists, the member may "peaceably withdraw . . . without attempting to make any schism," and seek fellowship in some other body.

These principles also apply to church members. While church members are not voting members of the courts of the church, Presbyterian bodies usually make provision for such persons to express objections to or concerns with actions of church courts.[59] If a church member finds himself in conscientious disagreement with a decision of a church court, and receives no satisfaction from that court, and if the matter is one that is determined to be "indispensable in doctrine, or Presbyterian government," the church member is free peaceably, not schismatically, to seek transfer of his membership to some other body.

THE RELATION OF CHURCH COURTS TO ONE ANOTHER

We have so far seen that Scripture understands the church to be broader and higher than the local congregation. Scripture speaks of the church at the local, regional, and universal levels. Furthermore, congregations are "connected together in government."[60] We have given some attention to the government of the church at both the congregational and the supra-congregational levels.

One question remains—how are the courts of the church related to one another? Scripture tells us that the church is governed at the congregational level by the session, and at higher levels by representative assemblies of elders. But how do the session and these higher courts relate to one another?

59. As, for instance, in the provision of "complaint." *BCO* 43–1.
60. Peck, *Notes on Ecclesiology*, 194.

Two popular answers understand the powers of one court to derive from the powers of another court. One answer we may term "top down." This view understands the powers of session to derive from presbytery, or the powers of session and presbytery to derive from general assembly. The other view we may term "bottom up." This view understands the powers of presbytery and general assembly to derive from session. Lefferts Loetscher, for instance, understands these positions to be two leading alternatives in historical Presbyterianism.

> An important feature of the first presbytery was that it was organized "from the ground up" not "from the top down" as was the Presbyterianism of Scotland which had been adopted by Parliament and implemented by the General Assembly. In America, on the contrary, the higher judicatories were created by the lower, establishing the more democratic nature of American Presbyterianism, and strengthening the concept that undelegated power remain in the presbyteries and not in the higher judicatories.[61]

Assessing the historical accuracy of this conclusion is beyond the scope of our discussion. We reference it simply to show two conventional ways in which some Presbyterians have understood the church courts to relate to one another. What these two views have in common is that both understand certain church courts to be the creatures of other church courts. This relationship can suggest that the powers of one court are granted to that court by another court. On this view, the powers of one court, properly speaking, are derivative of another court.

There are at least two problems with stating the relationships of church courts in this way. First, this view can claim that church power resides in a court of origination, and that other courts derive their power from this court. We have seen, however, that all church power derives from Christ. When a court legitimately exercises church power, it exercises power that Christ has given it, not power that another court has given it.

61. Loetscher, *A Brief History*, 72–73.

A second problem with this view is that it fails adequately to convey Scripture's teaching concerning the unity of the church. Peck nicely summarizes what we have already seen on this point.

> If all the communicants of the Presbyterian Church of the United States could meet for worship in the same place, they might and should be under the government of the same session; but as this is impossible, they are broken up into single congregations, each with its own session. But in order to preserve the unity, all these single or local presbyteries are ultimately combined by representation in one presbytery, which we call the General Assembly, passing through the intermediate states of classical and synodical presbyteries.[62]

What are the implications of this understanding of the unity of the church for the way in which we conceive the courts of the church to relate to one another? It means that the courts do not exist in hierarchical subordination, "one order of clergy rising above another." There is subordination, to be sure, but it is "a smaller body to a larger body of officers of the same order—the smaller constituting a part of the larger."[63]

At least two conclusions follow from this understanding of the relationship of the courts of the church. First, as the PCA's *Book of Church Order* states, "all Church courts are one in nature, constituted of the same elements, possessed inherently of the same kinds of rights and powers."[64] Courts, in other words, do not derive their powers from other courts "in a descending scale." Each court "is clothed with all the powers of government." As Peck further observes, "this is an important principle to the freedom and independence of church courts."[65]

Why, then, do we have multiple church courts? Why is it that most Presbyterian churches assign certain responsibilities to one court and not to another? Why, for instance, does presbytery and not session

---

62. Peck, *Notes on Ecclesiology*, 204.
63. Ibid.
64. *BCO* 11–3.
65. Peck, *Notes on Ecclesiology*, 205.

or general assembly examine candidates for the ministry? The answer is not because presbytery has an inherent power that session or general assembly lacks. The answer is found in a fuller citation of the reference that we cited above from the PCA's *Book of Church Order*: "All Church courts are one in nature, constituted of the same elements, possessed inherently of the same kinds of rights and powers, *and differing only as the Constitution may provide*." In the PCA, the "sphere of action of each court" has been "distinctly defined" as follows.

> The Session exercises jurisdiction over a single church, the Presbytery over what is common to the ministers, Sessions, and churches within a prescribed district, and the General Assembly over such matters as concern the whole Church. The jurisdiction of these courts is limited by the express provisions of the Constitution.[66]

Thus, as Peck observes, "the sphere of the several courts, therefore, in matters of original jurisdiction is not determined by the places they occupy in the scale, but by the definitions of the constitution."[67] In the PCA and many other Presbyterian bodies, church courts, by constitutional provision, take up matters suitable to the extent of the jurisdiction that they exercise.[68]

May we say more about the respective constitutional limitations of the jurisdiction of these courts? In the PCA, "the lower courts are subject to the review and control of the higher courts, in regular gradation," and these provisions of review and control are expressly enumerated.[69] Even so, the courts of the church are "not separate and independent tribunals," but in "mutual relation, and every act of jurisdiction is the act of the whole Church performed by it through the appropriate organ."[70]

---

66. *BCO* 11–4. Recall that *BCO* 11–2 describes ecclesiastical jurisdiction as "only ministerial and declarative, and relates to the doctrines and precepts of Christ, to the order of the Church, and to the exercise of discipline."

67. Peck, *Notes on Ecclesiology*, 205.

68. This point was urged in the seventeenth century by the authors of *Jus Divinum*; see especially page 198.

69. *BCO* 11–4. For the provisions for review and control, see *BCO* 39.

70. Ibid.

We may summarize this discussion using Peck's dictum that "the power of the whole is in every part, and the power of the whole is over the *power* of every part."[71] Each church court has inherently all the powers that any court of the church possesses—"the power of the whole is in every part." The courts of the church, however, are not autonomous or independent. The lower courts are subject to the review and control of the higher courts, in regular gradation, according to the provisions of the church's constitution—"the power of the whole is over the *power* of every part."[72]

Let us offer one illustration of the practical importance of these principles. In many Presbyterian denominations, General Assembly not infrequently appoints a committee to study a matter of some interest or concern to the denomination.[73] These committees represent some of the best scholarship and wisdom that the denomination has to offer. The papers that they draft and present to the Assembly are incalculably helpful to a church seeking clarity and insight into questions or difficulties that lie before her. As such, they rightly carry moral authority within the church.

When the Assembly receives such a study paper from a committee, what is the ecclesiastical status of such a report? It is not uncommon in the PCA to hear such papers described as "the official PCA position on _____." These papers, received by a single vote of the Assembly, come to assume within the church quasi-constitutional authority.

71. Peck, *Notes on Ecclesiology*, 205, emphasis Peck's; cf. "Worldly Amusements," in *Miscellanies*, 2:335.

72. As Peck notes on this latter phrase, "The general assembly has no power directly *over the part*, but only over the *power* of the part, which implies that the part has a power" (*Notes on Ecclesiology*, 206). Peck illustrate the point thus: "The question has always been . . . whether the whole is simply a great wheel, of which the parts are only spokes, or whether it be a wheel of which the parts are *also* wheels, each having a sphere and movement of its own, yet moving in subordination to the movement of the great wheel." "Worldly Amusements," in *Miscellanies*, 2:336.

73. For the PCA, these have been collected as *PCA Digest,* vol. 2: *PCA Position Papers*, ed. Paul R. Gilchrest, 2 vols. (Atlanta: Office of the Stated Clerk of the General Assembly of the Presbyterian Church in America, 1993), and *PCA Digest,* vol. 3: *PCA Position Papers, 1994–1998* (Atlanta: Office of the Stated Clerk of the General Assembly of the Presbyterian Church in America, 1998). A complete gathering of these papers is currently available online at the website of the PCA Historical Center, www.pcahistory.org.

There are problems with this understanding of study committee reports.[74] One practical problem is that lower courts (sessions, presbyteries) sometimes decline to form their own considered judgments on certain matters when they are called upon to do so. They defer, instead, to the Assembly and its study committee. Such a course of action may reflect an undue deference on the part of a lower court to a higher court. Each church court, we have seen, is "possessed inherently of the same kinds of right and powers, and differing only as the Constitution may provide." "Courts of original jurisdiction" have "the power of judgment, both as to law and fact." This power of judgment "can only be overruled and set aside by a *judicial decision* of the higher court upon a cause regularly (legally, constitutionally) brought up from a lower."[75] As helpful and as beneficial as Assembly-level study committee reports are, they are no substitute for lower courts exercising their constitutionally-acknowledged powers with respect to matters that are properly before them.[76]

In conclusion, the courts of the church exist because Christ in the Scriptures has made provision for them and for their work. They are an important way in which the unity of the church is given visible expression. The nature of the interrelation of the courts of the church means that each court should undertake its responsibilities with seriousness and care. Each court must do so because its jurisdictional actions are those of the whole church, subject to provisions of review and control. Each court must do so because it stands under the gaze of Christ and is, in the final analysis, accountable to the only Head and King of the Church.

74. Not least of which is the fact that, in the PCA, the Constitution may not be amended by a single vote of one General Assembly.

75. Peck, "Worldly Amusements," in *Miscellanies*, 2:335.

76. "Every court has the right to resolve questions of doctrine and discipline seriously and reasonably proposed, and in general to maintain truth and righteousness, condemning erroneous opinions and practices which tend to the injury of the peace, purity, or progress of the Church." *BCO* 11–4.

6

CONCLUSION

We have been considering Scripture's teaching on the government of the church. As we bring this study to a close, it may be helpful to step back and ask once again why we have devoted time and energy to considering what, at first glance, may seem mundane, unimportant, or even a distraction from the real business of the church. After all, one might ask, can church government really compare with evangelism or missions? Perhaps church government is a necessary evil—something to be tolerated but not cherished.

Let us remind ourselves of something that we saw in the Introduction. Church government is a pillar in the edifice of our Reformed and Presbyterian heritage. From Calvin into the twentieth century, our Reformed ancestors prized, studied, and devoted themselves to the government of the church. The reason for this often intense dedication is because the church's government is inseparably connected with the church's only Head and King, Jesus Christ.

Consider this historical meditation on the reign of Christ.

Jesus Christ, upon whose shoulders the government is, whose name is called Wonderful Counsellor, the mighty God, The everlasting Father, The Prince of Peace; of the increase of whose government and peace there shall be no end; who sits upon the throne of David, and upon his kingdom, to order it, and to establish it with judgment and justice, from henceforth, even for ever; having all power given unto him in heaven and in earth by the Father, who raised him from the dead, and set him at his own right hand, far above all principalities and power, and might, and dominion, and every name that is named, not only in this world, but also in that which is to come, and put all things under his feet, and gave him to be head over all things to the church, which is his body, the fulness of him that filleth all in all: he being ascended up far above all heavens, that he might fill all things, received gifts for his church, and gave officers necessary for the edification of his church, and perfecting of his saints.[1]

As we saw in chapter 2, critical to Old Testament expectation was the hope of God's worldwide, redemptive dominion. The New Testament announces that the redemptive rule and reign of God has arrived in the Son of God, Jesus Christ. When the angel Gabriel announces to Mary that she will be the mother of Jesus, he says of Jesus, "He will be great and will be called the Son of the Most High. And the Lord God will give to him the throne of his father David, and he will reign over the house of Jacob forever, and of his kingdom there will be no end" (Luke 1:32–33). When Jesus is born, the angels announce to the shepherds, "For unto you is born this day in the city of David a Savior, who is Christ the Lord" (Luke 2:11). The magi come looking for the "king of the Jews" and "worship[ed] him" (Matt. 2:2, 8).

The great theme of Jesus' ministry is the kingdom of God. His Galilean ministry begins with the announcement, "The time is fulfilled, and the kingdom of God is at hand; repent and believe in the gospel" (Mark 1:15). After his resurrection, Jesus tells his disciples that "all authority in heaven and on earth has been given to me" (Matt. 28:18). As Peter proclaimed on the day of Pentecost to the Jews gathered in Je-

---

1. "The Preface" to "The Form of Presbyterial Church-Government and of Ordination of Ministers" (1645). This document was "agreed upon by the Assembly of Divines at Westminster, with the assistance of commissioners from the Church of Scotland," and was approved by the General Assembly of the Church of Scotland in 1645. For the whole document, see *Westminster Confession of Faith* (Glasgow: Free Presbyterian Publications, 1958), 395–416.

rusalem, upon Jesus' resurrection he was "therefore exalted at the right hand of God" (Acts 2:33).

Jesus is no absentee ruler. He declares that he is with his people to the end of the age (Matt. 28:20). He is not only present with his people, but he also now rules over them. The apostles glory in the present reign of Jesus, as he is "head over all things to the church, which is his body, the fullness of him who fills all in all" (Eph. 1:22–23). As head of the church, Jesus "received gifts for His church, and gave all offices necessary for the edification of His Church and the perfecting of His saints."[2] Church government is a gift of the risen and reigning Jesus to the church, and perpetually reminds the church that Jesus is on his throne.

This present reign of Jesus is the church's present joy in the face of sorrow, and consolation in the face of trial and tribulation. Scripture assures us that "he must reign until he has put all his enemies under his feet," and that the "last enemy to be destroyed is death" (1 Cor. 15:25–26; cf. Heb. 2:8).

The present reign of Christ is also the church's present hope. The present reign of Jesus reminds us that there is more to come. When Jesus returns at the end of the age, he will return "in the clouds of heaven with power and great glory" (Matt. 24:30). Appearing in royal splendor, he will thoroughly defeat all his enemies (Rev. 19:11–21), and judge the world in righteousness (Acts 17:31).

Biblical church government, then, is a tremendous pillar and support to the church's faith, a signpost of the church's great hope. Church government reminds us that Jesus is presently on his throne, ruling over all things for the sake of his church. It assures us that Jesus will return in glory at the last day.

The day-to-day workings of church government, however, can be difficult and sometimes unpleasant. Church government, sadly, has been the occasion of Christians wounding and being wounded by other Christians. Temptations to discouragement and cynicism abound. We

---

2. "The King and Head of the Church," section 1 of "Preface to the *Book of Church Order*," *BCO*. This statement is an adaptation of the above-quoted "Preface" to the "Form of Presbyterial-Church Government."

can easily assume a posture of resigned indifference toward the government of the church. It is particularly on such occasions that we must remember that biblical church government is the visible expression of Jesus' present reign, and that church government is Jesus' good and wise provision for the gathering and upbuilding of his church. Biblical church government is itself good, and Jesus works good through it for his church.

To understand the government of the church is to know and to glorify our Lord Jesus Christ. If you are a church officer, then demonstrate your love for your Savior by dedicating yourself afresh to your office and its responsibilities. Is there some responsibility of yours that you have let slide? Is there an area where, as a church officer, you could be more diligent and careful? Make an effort to learn the principles and practices of biblical church government even better than you do now—not to be puffed up, but to edify the church. Go out of your way to encourage and support your fellow officers, especially those whose work often goes unnoticed or unappreciated, or those who are suffering unjustly for their faithfulness to duty. Pray fervently that the Spirit of Christ would use the faithful labors of you and your fellow officers for the good of Christ's flock. Work with your fellow officers to inform the church of the work of the courts of the church. This will show the congregation how seriously you take your responsibilities as a church officer, and simultaneously impress upon them the importance of the church's work.

If you are not a church officer, then show your love for Jesus by praying for the officers of the church and their work. Take the time and effort to encourage them. Do you tell them or write to them how much you appreciate their hard and often unseen work? Show respect for your church officers—in the way that you speak of them and to them, and in the way that you treat them. Model to your spouse, your children, and your grandchildren how to respect, honor, and encourage the officers of the church. Stay abreast of the work of the courts of the church. Make an effort to pray for the business that is before the session, the presbytery, and the General Assembly, and for the men who will be undertaking that work. Pray too that God would gift godly men for church office. Are you on the lookout in your congregation for suitable candidates for church office?

Such attention to the government of the church is inseparable from the believer's discipleship. To show concern for the church is to show concern for Jesus. To seek the good of the church is to seek the glory of Christ. To care about and to be zealous for the government of the church is to prize and to cherish the reign of Jesus. May the Spirit of Christ work in his church increasing zeal for and attention to the government of the church until the day when Jesus "delivers the kingdom to God the Father after destroying every rule and every authority and power," and God will be "all in all" (1 Cor. 15:24, 28).

7

CHURCH GOVERNMENT: A SELECT AND ANNOTATED BIBLIOGRAPHY

One of the greatest challenges to recovering the riches of historical Presbyterian reflection on church government is bibliographical accessibility. Much of this literature is at least a century old, has not been reprinted, and is housed almost exclusively in theological libraries. In the last decade or so, such websites as Google Books and Internet Archive have partially rectified this challenge. Many libraries are digitizing their holdings and making them accessible to anyone with an Internet connection.

Even so, the Internet provides these materials to individuals who look for them. How does one even learn of these materials' existence? Part of the burden of this book has been to reacquaint Presbyterian audiences with this part of their heritage. To assist intrepid readers who want to track down these works and to read further, I have compiled the following bibliography. I have tried to focus on works that were and continue to be regarded as important to this discussion. Many of them have been quoted in this book. For ease of reference, I have arranged these books under a few topical headings. I have also supplied brief annotations to help contemporary readers understand something of the content and importance of the work in question.

Careful readers will note that for the sake of space I have omitted books addressing related but distinct areas of concern: Presbyterian denominational history (including the many splits and mergers among many Presbyterian ecclesiastical bodies, and the theological issues that sometimes occasioned those splits and mergers), the regulative principle of worship, the sacraments, preaching, subscription to subordinate standards, church discipline, and pastoral theology. I have omitted the many nineteenth-century journals in which discussions and debates relating to church polity so often transpired. I have also opted not to include Presbyterian-authored commentaries on such books as Acts and the Pastoral Epistles.

At the outset, I need to make special mention of two resources in particular: John Calvin's *Institutes of the Christian Religion*[1] and Francis Turretin's *Institutes of Elenctic Theology*.[2] These two resources have exercised widespread influence on generations of Reformed and Presbyterians, not least in the area of church government. No reader who has not at least acquainted himself with book 4 of Calvin's *Institutes* and locus 18 of Turretin's *Institutes* can fully appreciate our tradition's discussions of church polity.

A valuable online resource is a website maintained by the PCA Historical Center. Visitors may find at this site many historical materials relating to Presbyterian church government and church history. Those particularly interested in the history and development of the PCA's *Book of Church Order* will find a wealth of information here.

My hope is that this bibliography will accomplish two goals. First, that it will give you a hint of the depth and fullness of Presbyterian reflection on the Scripture's teaching on church government. Second, that it will goad you to study these resources and to carry on—perhaps even to advance—this rich conversation in our own day: all to the upbuilding of the church, and to the glory of the church's only Head and King, Jesus Christ.

1. John Calvin, *Institutes of the Christian Religion*, ed. John T. McNeill, trans. Ford Lewis Battles, 2 vols. (Philadelphia: Westminster, 1960).
2. Francis Turretin, *Institutes of Elenctic Theology*, ed. James T. Dennison Jr., trans. George M. Giger, 3 vols. (Phillipsburg, NJ: P&R Publishing, 1992–97).

BOOKS OF CHURCH ORDER

The Book of Church Order of the Presbyterian Church in America. 6th ed. Lawrenceville, GA: The Committee for Christian Education and Publications, 2010. The most recent edition of the PCA's *Book of Church Order.* The *BCO* is often amended annually. Amendments are available through the PCA's Committee for Christian Education and Publications.

The Book of Church Order of the Orthodox Presbyterian Church. Willow Grove, PA: The Committee on Christian Education of the Orthodox Presbyterian Church, 2011. The most recent edition of the OPC's *Book of Church Order.*

Ramsay, F. P. *An Exposition of the Form of Government and the Rules of Discipline of the Presbyterian Church in the United States.* Richmond, VA: Presbyterian Committee of Publication, 1898. Frequently quoted by Smith (2007), this work is a section-by-section commentary on the PCUS's *Book of Church Order.* Helpful in understanding both the rationale for and historical pedigree of many provisions of contemporary Presbyterian church government.

Smith, Morton. *Commentary on the Book of Church Order of the Presbyterian Church in America.* 6th ed. Taylors, SC: Presbyterian Press, 2007. A section-by-section commentary on the PCA's *Book of Church Order* by a founding father of the PCA, and longtime stated clerk of the denomination. Valuable both in helping the reader to understand the principles at work in various provisions of the *BCO* and in setting many portions of the *BCO* in historical perspective.

DIGESTS

A digest is a selective collection of the actions of a court of the church. Generally, these collections are topically arranged and cover a set period of time. In so "digesting" thousands of pages of church minutes, they make those minutes practically accessible to the church. These digests provide a treasure trove of information for those interested, for

155

instance, in how church courts interpreted their ecclesiastical constitution. Many particulars of church government are addressed in these works. Entries in the list below are arranged in rough chronological order. The nineteenth-century entries have been further grouped geographically.

Records of the Presbyterian Church in the United States of America, 1706–1788. 1841. Reprint, New York: Arno Press & The New York Times, 1969. In light of the relative brevity of minutes from eighteenth-century American Presbyterian higher courts, these particular minutes have been printed in their entirety. This collection includes the minutes of the Presbytery of Philadelphia (1706–16), the Synod of Philadelphia (1717–58), the Synod of New York (1745–58), and the Synod of Philadelphia and New York (1758–88).

Baird, Samuel J. *A Collection of the Acts, Deliverances and Testimonies of the Supreme Judicatory of the Presbyterian Church from Its Origin in America to the Present Time, with Notes and Documents, Explanatory and Historical.* Philadelphia: Presbyterian Board of Publication, 1856. This digest encompasses the actions of the General Assembly of the Presbyterian Church from 1706 to the 1850s (after the Old School/New School split of 1836–37, Baird's work follows only the minutes of the Old School Presbyterian Church). The work is substantial (856 pages) and meticulously arranged and indexed. Invaluable for gleaning the wisdom of past Assemblies concerning a host of issues and questions facing the church.

Nicolassen, G. F. *A Digest of the Acts and Proceedings of the General Assembly of the Presbyterian Church in the United States Revised Down to and Including Acts of the General Assembly of 1922.* Richmond, VA: Presbyterian Committee of Publication, 1923. Sometimes known as "Alexander's Digest" (W. A. Alexander originally prepared the digest of the PCUS Assembly in 1887). At 1,158 pages, this work provides a comprehensive overview of the work of the PCUS Assembly from 1861 to 1922. (The PCUS was formed after the Presbyterian Church split into Northern and Southern bodies in

1861. The PCUS is sometimes known as the Southern Presbyterian Church, and is the body from which the PCA emerged.) Subsequent digests were published in 1944 and 1965.

Leslie, J. D. *Presbyterian Law and Procedure in the Presbyterian Church in the United States.* Richmond, VA: Presbyterian Committee of Publication, 1930. Authored by the (then) stated clerk of the PCUS, this work seeks to "bring together in logical form and in brief compass all the laws and rules of the Church relating to every phase of its government, work, and worship" (p. 7). It is, by design, an abridgment of Alexander's and Nicolassen's digests (Leslie has also consulted the minutes of the PCUS through 1929). It is structured according to the (then) Form of Government of the PCUS. Note also the subsequent effort by P. J. Garrison Jr., *Presbyterian Laws and Procedures: The Presbyterian Church, U.S.* (Richmond, VA: John Knox Press, 1953). Leslie's work in effect complements the effort of J. A. Hodge (1884).

Moore, William E. *The Presbyterian Digest of 1886. A Compend of the Acts and Deliverances of the General Assembly of the Presbyterian Church in the United States of America.* Philadelphia: Presbyterian Board of Publication, 1886. At 876 pages, a substantial supplement and extension of Baird (1856). Moore first prepared his digest three years after the Old School and New School Presbyterian Churches (North) had reunited in 1870. He revised it in 1886. This work, then, is valuable in two respects. First, it extends Baird's efforts by three decades. Second, it allows readers to survey decisions of the New School Presbyterian Church (1838–69) not recorded in Baird. Readers interested in the acts and deliverances of the PCUS, or the Southern Presbyterian Church, should consult Nicolassen (1923).

Hodge, J. Aspinwall. *What Is Presbyterian Law as Defined by the Church Courts?* 7th ed., rev. and enl. Philadelphia: Presbyterian Board of Publication and Sabbath-School Work, 1884. J. Aspinwall Hodge was a Northern Presbyterian pastor and nephew of Princeton Theological Seminary professor Charles Hodge. This invaluable work surveys the contents of the Form of Government of the Northern

Presbyterian Church in question-and-answer form. It does so with reference to the acts and deliverances of the General Assembly of the Northern Presbyterian Church. It is therefore a hybrid of a commentary on the church's Form of Government and a digest of the actions of its Assembly. Compare the similar and later effort of Leslie (1930).

Gilchrist, Paul J., ed. *Documents of Synod*. New Castle, DE: Reformed Presbyterian Church, Evangelical Synod, 1982. The RPC(ES), by a process known as "joining and receiving," joined the PCA in 1982. This volume contains "study papers and actions" of this body from 1965 to 1982. A helpful "index to the synodical actions" of the RPC(ES) concludes the volume. For those interested in PCA history and polity, this work is an important resource.

———. *PCA Digest: 1973–1993. A Digest of the Minutes of the General Assembly of the Presbyterian Church in America*. 2 vols. Atlanta: Office of the Stated Clerk of the General Assembly of the Presbyterian Church in America, 1993. A digest of the actions of the PCA's General Assembly in the first two decades of the denomination's existence. The first volume is in four parts: "assembly actions; interpretations of the constitution; judicial cases; bylaws, manuals, and guidelines." The second volume is a collection of position papers drafted by committees appointed by the Assembly. Some papers are followed by a list of relevant recommendations that the Assembly adopted.

———. *PCA Position Papers: 1994–1998*. Vol. 3 of *PCA Digest*. Atlanta: Office of the Stated Clerk of the General Assembly of the Presbyterian Church in America, 1998. A continuation of Gilchrist (1993). This volume contains Assembly-level position papers from 1994 to 1998, and a combined index of Gilchrist (1993) and this work. Gilchrist's warning regarding the ecclesiastical standing of these position papers is salutary: "It needs to be pointed out that when quoting the position papers, caution should be exercised as to whether they were merely received or if they were adopted as the action of General Assembly. Even when adopted, these papers and decisions reflect the pious advice of that particular General Assembly and have no constitutional force unless changes were adopted in the *Book of Church Order* or other standards of the Church" (1993:3).

SURVEYS

Hall, David W., and Joseph H. Hall. *Paradigms in Polity: Classic Readings in Reformed and Presbyterian Church Government.* Grand Rapids: Eerdmans, 1994. An anthology of selections from leading historical Reformed and Presbyterian works on church polity. After the editors' introduction follow selections from "Continental Europe and Reformation Polities," "Dutch Reformed Polities," "Scottish and British Polities," and "North American Polities." Helpful introductions precede the selections, and a nice bibliographical essay concludes the volume. For a reader interested in the historical pedigree and development of Presbyterian church government, this volume is an important place to begin.

Pre-1900: The British Isles

Entries in the list below are arranged in rough chronological order. The nineteenth-century entries have been further grouped geographically.

Jus Divinum Regiminis Ecclesiastici, or The Divine Right of Church-Government, Originally Asserted by the Ministers of Sions College, London, December, 1646. Revised and edited by David Hall. Reprint, Dallas: Naphtali, 1995. Widely regarded to have been authored by certain members of the Westminster Assembly, this work is an early and foundational exposition and defense of *jus divinum* (divine right) Presbyterianism. One of the most robust biblical treatments of *jus divinum* Presbyterianism available.

Bannerman, James. *The Church of Christ: A Treatise on the Nature, Powers, Ordinances, Discipline, and Government of the Christian Church.* 2 vols. Edinburgh: T&T Clark, 1868. Reprint, Edinburgh: Banner of Truth, 1960. Arguably the most thorough Presbyterian text on the doctrine of the church. Bannerman's son, D. Douglas Bannerman (see below), compiled these two volumes from lectures that James Bannerman had delivered to his ministerial students in New College, Free Church of Scotland. Bannerman leaves few departments of the doctrine of the church untouched. Particularly helpful is Bannerman's engagement of non-Presbyterian forms of church government.

Cunningham, William. *Historical Theology: A Review of the Principal Doctrinal Discussions in the Christian Church Since the Apostolic Age*. 3rd ed. 2 vols. Edinburgh: T&T Clark, 1870. Reprint, Edinburgh: Banner of Truth, 1960. A contemporary of Bannerman, Cunningham served as principal and professor of church history, New College, Edinburgh. While much of this work covers areas extending well beyond the doctrine of the church, Cunningham's chapters on "The Church" (1:9–42), "The Council of Jerusalem" (1:43–78), "The Civil and Ecclesiastical Authorities" (1:390–412), "Church Government" (2:514–56), and "The Erastian Controversy" (2:557–87) merit study. Like Bannerman, Cunningham assists the reader in setting the doctrine of the church in historical-theological context.

Cunningham, William. *Discussions on Church Principles: Popish, Erastian, and Presbyterian*. Edinburgh: T&T Clark, 1863. A posthumous collection of Cunningham's published and unpublished material on the doctrine of the church (p. iii). Particularly helpful is Cunningham's article "Church Power" (pp. 235–56).

MacPherson, John. *Presbyterianism*. Edinburgh: T&T Clark, 1882. Part of the T&T Clark series Handbooks for Bible Classes, *Presbyterianism* offers a luminous and succinct statement (154 pp.) of Presbyterian church government. MacPherson, a Free Church minister, was also the author of a brief commentary on the Westminster Confession of Faith and a famous series of lectures on the doctrine of the church in Scottish theology.

Bannerman, D. Douglas. *The Scripture Doctrine of the Church Historically and Exegetically Considered—The Eleventh Series of the Cunningham*

Lectures. Edinburgh: T&T Clark, 1887. Reprint, Grand Rapids: Baker, 1976. D. Douglas Bannerman was a Free Church minister and the son of James Bannerman (above). The value of this work is in its presentation of a fundamentally biblical-theological treatment of the Scripture's teaching on the church. Bannerman begins with "The Church in the Time of Abraham" and concludes with "The Gentile Christian Church . . . Antioch and Rome."

Witherow, Thomas. *The Apostolic Church: Which Is It? An Enquiry at the Oracles of God as to Whether Any Existing Form of Church Government Is of Divine Right.* 5th rev. ed. Glasgow: Andrew Elliot, 1881. Reprint, Glasgow: Free Presbyterian Publications, 1990. A brief and widely reprinted statement of basic principles of Presbyterian church government (an abridgment appears in Hall and Hall). The author served as professor of church history, Magee College, Londonderry.

———. *The Form of the Christian Temple: Being a Treatise on the Constitution of the New Testament Church.* Edinburgh: T&T Clark, 1889. A more substantial treatment (468 pp.) of church government by the author of *The Apostolic Church: Which Is It?* The work is divided into three parts: "Book I: Temporary Agencies [of the church]," "Book II: Divine and Permanent Elements [of the church]," and "Book III: Human Additions [to the church]." Long out of print, this work merits reprinting.

Killen, William D. *The Framework of the Church: A Treatise on Church Government.* Edinburgh: T&T Clark, 1890. Killen was a nineteenth century Irish Presbyterian. He served as professor of ecclesiastical history and pastoral theology at, and later president of, the Irish Assembly's College, Belfast, and principal of the Presbyterian Theological Faculty, Ireland. This 355-page treatise on the church's government is divided into four parts: "The Church and Its Government," "Congregationalism," "Prelacy," and "Presbytery." One strength of Killen's work is its concern to address the historical evidence from the early centuries of the church's history (see also Killen's *The Ancient Church,* ed. John Hall [New York: Anson D. F. Randolph & Company, 1883]). Long out of print, this work merits reprinting.

Pre-1900: The United States

The first two entries below were published before the Presbyterian Church split along geographical lines. Most of the subsequent entries were published after this split and so have been grouped geographically.

Mason, John Mitchell. *Essays on the Church of God: In Which the Doctrines of Church Membership and Infant Baptism Are Fully Discussed.* 1843. Reprint, Taylors, SC: Presbyterian Press, 2005. John Mitchell Mason was an influential minister in the Associate Reformed Church at the turn of the nineteenth century. This work aims to give "a detailed but succinct account of the Church of God, embracing the chief questions concerning its nature, members, officers, order, worship, and the points directly connected with them" (p. 1). Dabney, Peck, and McGill were only three of the many American Presbyterians who acknowledged the importance of these essays for a biblical understanding of the church and its government. Recently reprinted, these essays are included in both editions of Mason's *Works* (1832, 1849).

Miller, Samuel. *Presbyterianism, the Truly Primitive and Apostolic Constitution of the Church of Christ.* Philadelphia: Presbyterian Board of Publication, 1840. Miller, the first professor of ecclesiastical history and church government at Princeton Theological Seminary, authored this relatively brief statement and defense of the history, doctrine, government, and worship of the Presbyterian Church. Frequently reprinted throughout the nineteenth century, Miller's tract earned the respect and admiration of later Presbyterians, both Northern and Southern. For modern readers looking for an introduction to the principles of Presbyterian church government, Miller's piece is an ideal starting point.

Peck, Thomas E. *Notes on Ecclesiology.* 2nd ed. Richmond, VA: Presbyterian Committee of Publication, 1892. Reprint, Greenville, SC: Presbyterian Press, 2005. Peck served at Union Theological Seminary (Virginia) from 1860 to 1893. He first taught church history and government and then, succeeding Dabney, theology. This work consists essentially of Peck's lecture notes in church government. It is the most thorough and wide-ranging statement on the subject by a Southern Presbyterian, and indispensable for understanding the Scripture's teaching on the government of the church.

————. *Miscellanies of Thomas E. Peck.* 3 vols. Richmond, VA: Presbyterian Committee of Publication, 1895–97. Reprint, Edinburgh: Banner of Truth, 1999. The *Miscellanies* are Peck's journal articles, sermons, and notes posthumously collected and published. Some of these pieces are valuable statements of aspects of the doctrine of church government. "Church and State" (2:266–89) by no means reproduces Peck's statement of the subject in his *Notes*. "The Powers of Our Several Church Courts" (2:331–60) is a definitive statement concerning the power of the church as exercised by its various courts. "Thornwell's Writings" (2:361–99, esp. 383–99) offers Peck's sympathetic survey and analysis of Thornwell's principles concerning the government of the church.

Robinson, Stuart. *The Church of God as an Essential Element of the Gospel.* Philadelphia: Joseph M. Wilson, 1858. Reprint, Willow Grove, PA: The Committee on Christian Education of the Orthodox Presbyterian Church, 2009. Robinson was a distinguished Presbyterian minister who briefly taught church government and pastoral theology at Danville (Kentucky) Theological Seminary, and served as moderator of the General Assembly of the PCUS in 1869. *The Church of God* originated as an "Inaugural Discourse . . . delivered before [the Danville Theological Seminary] during the sessions of the General Assembly at Lexington, Ky., in May, 1857." Long out of print, but now attractively reprinted, Robinson's *The Church of God* eloquently advances the thesis that the church is not incidental to God's one plan to save sinners through Christ. On the contrary, the church is central to the outworking of this one plan in redemptive history. Robinson's work, then, helpfully situates the doctrine of the church and of her government in biblical-theological context. It thus provides a valuable contemporary complement to Peck's *Notes on Ecclesiology*.

————. *Discourses of Redemption* . . . 4th American ed. Richmond, VA: Presbyterian Committee of Publication, 1866. Valuable in their own right as a redemptive-historical survey of Scripture, these *Discourses* have appended to them valuable "notes," two of which are "The Place of the Church in the Scheme of Redemption" and "The Relation of the Temporal and the Spiritual Powers Historically Considered: The Scoto-American Theory" (pp. 453–70; 474–88). As T. David Gordon has noted, this latter piece helpfully demonstrates the antecedents of the Southern Presbyterian doctrine of the spirituality of the church in Scottish Presbyterian theology.

Dabney, Robert L. *Discussions: Evangelical and Theological*. Vol. 2 of *Discussions*. Richmond, VA: Presbyterian Committee of Publication, 1891. Reprint, Edinburgh: Banner of Truth, 1967. Dabney, Virginia Presbyterian minister and longtime professor at Union Theological Seminary (Virginia), never published a systematic treatment of church government. But he has left a number of important pieces touching on the subject. Some of these pieces have been gathered in the second volume (of four) of Dabney's *Discussions*. "Theories of the Eldership" is a thorough and important statement of the "two-office" view of the eldership. "What Is Christian Union?" addresses what the unity of the church does (and does not) mean for ecclesiastical union and fellowship. "Wall Street Church Decision in the United States Supreme Court" offers Dabney's reflections on an important contemporary church-state question. Readers interested in learning more about Dabney's thoughts on the relationship between church and state should also consult his *Syllabus and Notes of the Course of Systematic and Polemic Theology Taught in Union Theological Seminary, Virginia*, 2nd rev. ed. (Richmond, VA: Shepperson & Graves, 1871; repr., Edinburgh: Banner of Truth, 1985), 862–87; and his *The Practical Philosophy: Being the Philosophy of the Feelings, of the Will, and of the Conscience, with the Ascertainment of Particular Rights and Duties* (Kansas City, MO: Hudson, Kimberly, 1897; repr., Harrisonburg, VA: Sprinkle Publications, 1984), 302–28.

Thornwell, James H. *Collected Writings of James Henley Thornwell: Ecclesiastical*. Vol. 4 of *Collected Writings*. Edited by John B. Adger and John L. Girardeau. Richmond, VA: Presbyterian Committee of Publication, 1873. Reprint, Edinburgh: Banner of Truth, 1974. Thornwell was an influential South Carolina Presbyterian minister and professor in the mid-nineteenth century. This volume of Thornwell's *Collected Writings* is a posthumous gathering of Thornwell's writings on the church. Noteworthy are Thornwell's defenses of the "two-office" view of the eldership (see pp. 43–142) and Thornwell's arguments against "church boards" (pp. 144–295). Also included in this volume is the influential "Address to All Churches of Christ" (pp. 446–64), which Thornwell authored and which the Southern Presbyterian Church subsequently adopted in 1861. This address remains a powerful and influential statement of the nature and mission of the church.

Smyth, Thomas. *The Complete Works of Rev. Thomas Smyth, D.D.* Edited by J. Wm. Flinn. 10 vols. Columbia, SC: R. L. Bryan, 1908. Smyth, a learned and prolific Presbyterian minister, emigrated from Ireland and served with distinction the Second Presbyterian Church, Charleston, South Carolina, from 1834 to 1873. Smyth's *Complete Works* did not receive wide circulation when they were first printed and have not been reprinted. As a result, they are difficult to find (a Table of Contents is currently available at the PCA Historical Center's website). Unlike many other Southern Presbyterians, Smyth adopted a "three-office" view of the ministry and defended (with Charles Hodge and others) "church boards." Many of Smyth's ecclesiological writings offer a defense of Presbyterianism against Prelacy. Volume 4 contains his "Ecclesiastical Catechism of the Presbyterian Church for the Use of Families, Bible Classes, and Private Members," for which Smyth is best known, and which helpfully gives expression to many principles of Presbyterian ecclesiology in accessible format.

Hodge, Charles. *Discussions in Church Polity: From the Contributions to the "Princeton Review."* New York: Charles Scribner's Sons, 1878.

A longtime professor at Princeton Theological Seminary, Charles Hodge published his three-volume *Systematic Theology* near the end of his life. According to Hodge's son, A. A. Hodge, Charles Hodge planned a fourth volume touching the doctrine of the church, but did not live to draft that volume. Hodge's ecclesiological articles, published in the *Princeton Theological Review* from 1835 to 1867, were bundled and, with Hodge's blessing, published in this roughly 540-page volume. While not a thorough statement of the doctrine of the church, Hodge's articles touch on many points of church government and represent an important Northern Presbyterian voice in the mid- to late nineteenth century.

————. *Constitutional History of the Presbyterian Church in the United States.* 2 vols. Philadelphia: Presbyterian Board of Publication, 1851. While technically a history of the American Presbyterian Church, Hodge's *Constitutional History* periodically reflects on some of the important questions relating to church government that arose during this period. Noteworthy in this connection is Hodge's discussion and analysis of the eighteenth-century Old/New Side split.

McGill, A. T. *Church Government: A Treatise Compiled from His Lectures in Theological Seminaries.* Philadelphia: Presbyterian Board of Publication and Sabbath-School Work, 1888. *Church Government* provides, in some respects, a (lengthier) counterpart to Peck's *Notes on Ecclesiology.* This work, as the subtitle indicates, comprises McGill's lectures in church government in their most mature form. McGill served Western Theological Seminary (Allegheny, Pennsylvania), Columbia Theological Seminary (South Carolina), and finally Princeton Theological Seminary, the latter from 1854 to 1883. "He was moderator of the General Assembly of the Presbyterian Church (Old School) in 1848, Permanent Clerk from 1850 to 1862, and Stated Clerk from 1862 to 1870" (Alfred Nevin, ed., *Encyclopaedia of the Presbyterian Church in the United States of America, Including the Northern and Southern Assemblies* [Philadelphia: Presbyterian Publishing, 1884], 495). One noteworthy feature of this work is its forty-page discussion of the deacon, including a defense of the deaconess.

166

Contemporary

The first four entries below were authored by faculty members of Westminster Theological Seminary and are arranged in rough chronological order. The latter two entries are more immediately related to the Presbyterian Church in America (PCA).

Murray, John. *The Collected Writings of John Murray: The Claims of Truth and Select Lectures in Systematic Theology.* Vols. 1 and 2 of *Collected Writings.* Carlisle, PA: Banner of Truth, 1977. Murray, professor of systematic theology at Westminster Theological Seminary from 1930 to 1966, never published a systematic theology or a treatise on the church. Many of his lectures and published articles, however, were posthumously assembled in this collection. The first two volumes contain pieces treating the doctrine of church government. Noteworthy are "The Church and Mission" (1:24–52); "The Relation of Church and State" (1:25–59), "Government in the Church of Christ" (1:260–68), "The Biblical Basis for Ecclesiastical Union" (1:269–72), "The Government of the Church" (2:336–44), "The Form of Government" (2:345–50), "Arguments against Term Eldership" (2:351–56), and "Office in the Church" (2:357–65).

Kuiper, R. B. *The Glorious Body of Christ.* Grand Rapids: Eerdmans, 1958. Like Clowney (1995), this book is one of the few twentieth-century examples of an extended Reformed statement on the church. Portions of it touch on the doctrine of church government. Although Kuiper's background was in the Reformed churches, he served as professor at Westminster Theological Seminary (Pennsylvania), and therefore had occasion both to interact with and to influence Presbyterian colleagues and students.

Clowney, Edmund P. "Distinctive Emphases in Presbyterian Church Polity." In *Pressing toward the Mark*, edited by Charles Dennison and Richard Gamble, 99–110. Philadelphia: The Committee for the Historian of the Orthodox Presbyterian Church, 1986. A brief twentieth-century statement of the principles underlying

Presbyterian church government by a longtime professor at, and later president of, Westminster Theological Seminary (Pennsylvania).

———. *The Church*. Downers Grove, IL: InterVarsity, 1995. While not a statement of Presbyterian church government per se, this work is a rare twentieth-century Presbyterian statement on the church. Clowney is particularly concerned to set the doctrine of the church in its biblical-theological context.

Cannada, Robert C., and W. Jack Williamson. *The Historic Polity of the PCA*. Greenville, SC: A Press, 1997. An influential treatment of church government by two founding fathers of the Presbyterian Church in America. Many of its multiple appendices helpfully give the reader access to historical statements of American Presbyterian polity.

Lucas, Sean M. *On Being Presbyterian: Our Beliefs, Practices, and Stories*. Phillipsburg, NJ: P&R Publishing, 2006. A widely read and non-technical statement of Presbyterian doctrine, worship, government, and history. Pages 132–48 offer a concise and selective survey of principles of Presbyterian polity and discuss their implementation in the Presbyterian Church in America.

INDEX OF SCRIPTURE

169

INDEX OF SUBJECTS AND NAMES